Rev. Joseph M. Vignos

THE PAPACY

IS VOLUME

81

OF THE

Twentieth Century Encyclopedia of Catholicism

UNDER SECTION

VIII

THE ORGANIZATION OF THE CHURCH

IT IS ALSO THE

12TH

VOLUME IN ORDER OF PUBLICATION

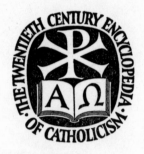

Edited by HENRI DANIEL-ROPS of the Académie Française

THE PAPACY

By *WLADIMIR D'ORMESSON*

Translated from the French by MICHAEL DERRICK

HAWTHORN BOOKS · PUBLISHERS · *New York*

First Edition, February, 1959

NIHIL OBSTAT

Hubertus Richards, S.T.L., L.S.S.

   Censor Deputatus

IMPRIMATUR

E. Morrogh Bernard,

   Vicarius Generalis

Westmonasterii, die X OCTOBRIS, MCMLVIII

The Library of Congress has catalogued this publication as follows:

Ormesson, Wladimir, *comte* d', 1888–
   The papacy. Translated from the French by Michael Derrick.
[1st ed.] New York, Hawthorn Books [1959]

   142 p. 21 cm. (The Twentieth century encyclopedia of Catholicism, v. 81. Section 8: The organization of the church)

   Includes bibliography.

---

   1. Papacy. (Series: The Twentieth century encyclopedia of Catholicism, v. 81)

BX1805.O713   262.1309   59–6740

CONTENTS

FOREWORD

When I was asked to write this volume about the Vicars of Christ, my first thought—which is always the best!—was to decline the honour. I am not an historian, still less an exegete. I did not feel myself qualified to do justice to the greatest and the longest history that the world has known. If finally I gave in it was on the understanding that nothing new was to be expected of me. To keep the book within reasonable dimensions it seemed to me that the best thing to do was to try to establish the origins of the papacy as clearly as possible, and then to define its position in the modern world. A single thread—I almost said a rainbow—would link the first ages of Christianity to our own time. Through these twenty centuries it would be enough to indicate the essential characteristics of the work of the popes.

I hope the reader may derive from this rough outline a desire to know more about the subject. In that event, he will have a very wide choice of authoritative works to introduce him to the history of the papacy.[1]

I would neither have begun nor completed this little book if I had not been encouraged, advised and enlightened by wise friends. In thanking them all I wish to express here my especial gratitude to Mgr Cristiani, whose experience has guided me, whose erudition has greatly helped me in my reading, and whose name ought to appear here alongside my own, so much do I owe to him. Perhaps he will allow me to inscribe it with gratitude at the beginning of these pages.

W. O.

[1] A select bibliography will be found at the end of this book.

CHAPTER I

THE PRIMACY OF PETER

It was in the year 29, fifteen days before the Passover. Jesus was coming from Capharnaum, where he had foretold the Eucharist. In danger from the agents of Herod Antipas who were listening to everything he said, our Lord was going towards Jerusalem by a roundabout way. He left the Lake of Genesareth and went in the direction of Caesarea Philippi, where one of the springs of the Jordan rises. Twelve of his disciples were with him, those who from that time were never again to leave him: Simon, the fisherman from Bethsaida; Andrew his brother; James and John, the sons of Zebedee; Philip and Nathanael, who was known also as Bar Tolmai, from the name of his father, an important man at Cana; Levi the publican who was surnamed Matthew, the God-given; James the Less, and Jude (who was known also as Thaddeus, or Lebbaeus), who were cousins of Jesus; Thomas, the twin, Simon, the Zealot; and finally Judas from Kerioth, the most recently joined of this faithful band.

These twelve disciples were only the few who remained. When he was going through Galilee, Judaea, Idumaea and the country beyond Jordan, Jesus had been followed by a large crowd. People had come from all parts, and even from the countries of Tyre and Sidon, to draw near to him, to listen to him. But almost all had left him; some from fear, others from weakness. Miracles, yes; these were very much desired; but the greatest thing of all, to conquer self by and for the love of God, what good was that? That was not what men asked of Jesus.

In one of the villages in the region of Safed, a halting-place on the journey back to the Holy City, the Master, that spring evening, assembled the last of his followers. He looked at them for a long while, and said to them, "Would you, too, go away?" "Lord," replied Peter, who spoke in the name of his companions, "to whom should we go? Thy words are the words of eternal life; we have learned to believe."

Jesus went to pray. Then he came back among his disciples and asked them this question, "Who do men say that I am?" They looked at one another. One by one they replied, "Some say John the Baptist, others Elias, others again, Jeremy or one of the old prophets that has returned to life." "And you," Jesus went on; "who do you say that I am?" Speaking again in the name of them all, Peter replied, "Thou art the Christ, the Son of the living God." Then Jesus said to him: "Blessed art thou, Simon son of Jona; it is not flesh and blood, it is my Father in heaven that has revealed this to thee. And I tell thee this in my turn, that thou art Peter, and it is upon this rock that I will build my church; and the gates of hell shall not prevail against it; and I will give to thee the keys of the kingdom of heaven; and whatever thou shalt bind on earth shall be bound in heaven; and whatever thou shalt loose on earth shall be loosed in heaven." (Matt. 16.17–19.) At the same time Jesus forbade his disciples to tell any man that he, Jesus, was the Christ.

Such are the essential words which conferred on Simon Peter the primacy among the disciples of Christ, and a special mission in the development of the Church. From these words, written in the sixteenth chapter of the Gospel of St Matthew, the papacy was born. They were to remain its basic charter through the centuries.

In the eleventh century in the East, in the sixteenth century in the West, Christian unity suffered two injuries which to this day nothing has been able to heal. The Eastern schism, foreshadowed by Photius towards the end of the ninth century and consummated by Michael Cerularius in 1054, separated a large number of Christians from the See of Peter. So it was also with the Protestant schism of which Martin Luther was the instigator. Only the Catholic Church, which includes today 472 million faithful throughout the world, did not cease and does not cease to recognize the Bishop of Rome as head of the Universal Church, and to honour him as the direct successor of Simon Peter.

On what arguments, for what reasons, in virtue of what facts do we Catholics hold to this conviction? Why do we say that Simon Peter represents not only the foundation-stone of the Christian edifice but the first head of Christ's Church? Why do we believe that the Church of Rome, of which he was the founder, has enjoyed a clear authority over the other Churches from the beginning of the Christian era? Why do we regard the successive heads of the Christian community in Rome, to whom the name of popes has been given since the sixth century, as so many successive heads of the Universal Church? Why does the Catholic world today proclaim that Pope John XXIII, now gloriously reigning, is the 258th successor of St Peter? These are the questions that I shall attempt to answer first. They go, if I may so express it, to the roots of the Catholic, Apostolic and Roman Church.

The *Tu es Petrus* of St Matthew's Gospel was not the first commission which Simon Peter received from the Master; or, more precisely, the way for that commission had already been prepared by a remarkable event.

We must go back a little in the public life of Jesus Christ—about two years—to find the first indication of the unique destiny reserved for the disciple known as Simon. Turn to the fourth Gospel, the Gospel of St John.

John the Baptist has begun to preach beside the Jordan. An unknown man comes to him among the others: it is Jesus of Nazareth. The prophet recognizes him at once. He points him out one day to two Galileans who have also come to receive baptism in the Jordan. "Look, this is the Lamb of God," he says to them. It is enough. Drawn by a power which they cannot explain, the two Galileans follow Jesus; they are overcome. One of them is called Andrew. He goes to find his elder brother, who is called Simon, and in a burst of enthusiasm says

to him, "We have discovered the Messias!" Simon, an im-
petuous Galilean, wants to see this discovery for himself. Led
by Andrew, he comes to Jesus; and, says the Gospel, Jesus
looks at this man whom he has never seen before and says the
moment he sees him, "Thou art Simon the son of Jona; thou
shalt be called Cephas."

This simple phrase changes everything. Henceforward Simon
will be Simon no more; he will be Cephas—an Aramaic name,
which means *Petrus*. A Protestant who not long ago studied
the meaning of this name, Professor O. Cullmann, has written:
"It is significant that it should have been possible to translate
the word *kepha* into Greek. This confirms that it was not a
proper name, for proper names cannot be translated." And to
give it its full meaning Professor Cullmann translates it by the
expression, "the Man-Rock". So Simon the son of Jona becomes
the Man-Rock. "The words which the Jews chose as surnames",
says Cullmann, "were usually intended to express a promise and
to impose an obligation on those who bore them."[1]

What is also remarkable, and fruitful already in compassion,
is that Peter, upon whom the Church is to be founded and who
receives this predestined name of the Man-Rock from the
Master, is not at all a person with a rock-like character. He is,
on the contrary, full of human weakness. He was to show
himself weak even to the extent of the denial in the courtyard
of the high priest. For all this, it is he who is chosen to guide
the Christian community, to receive here below the power to
bind and to loose whatever shall be bound and loosed in
heaven. Again we quote Professor O. Cullmann: "Peter", he
writes, "certainly had nothing of the 'Rock' about him so long
as Jesus was alive. On the contrary, one is surprised at his
weakness. Nothing better illustrates his character than the
occasion of the walking on the waters: impulsive, enthusiastic,
he does not hesitate, in his first ardour, to risk himself upon
the water when Jesus calls him; but his courage soon fails and
fear grips him. In the same way also he is the first to affirm
his fidelity to the Master and the first to deny him in the hour

[1] O. Cullmann, *Peter: Disciple, Apostle, Martyr.*

of danger." Peter is strong in the supernatural life; but without
that he is only a poor man like the others.

His preeminence among Christ's disciples is established, in
the eyes of the Catholic Church, by three fundamental texts.
These texts are found in the Gospels of St Matthew, St Luke
and St John—that is, in the only Gospels which were not
written, as was St Mark's, under the influence of Peter himself.

The first of these texts, and the most important, is that which
is to be found in Matthew (16.17–19), which I have already
quoted:

"And I tell thee this in thy turn, that thou art Peter, and it is
upon this rock that I will build my church; and the gates of hell
shall not prevail against it; and I will give to thee the keys of
the kingdom of heaven; and whatever thou shalt bind on earth
shall be bound in heaven; and whatever thou shalt loose on
earth shall be loosed in heaven."

It is the authority of this text that is invoked to establish the
primacy of Peter and his successors. Consequently three questions must be asked about it:

Is it authentic?

What powers does it promise to Peter?

Are these transmissible powers, and have they in fact been
transmitted to his successors?

Attempts have been made to cast doubt on the authenticity
of this text. Its clarity, its precision are such that it hardly
admits of any other interpretation than that of the Catholic
faith. It has also been maintained that it was interpolated at the
end of the second century or the beginning of the third, and
that what Matthew really heard Jesus say was no more than
the words: "Thou art Peter and the gates of hell shall not
prevail against thee." The phrase, "and it is upon this rock
that I will build my church", was introduced about this time,
so the argument goes, for temporal and political reasons.
However, since this theory was put forward it has been proved
that the version of St Matthew's Gospel accepted by the
Catholic Church is the same version that was known to Tatian

when he made his harmony of the four Gospels in the year 170, and therefore *before* the presumed date of the interpolation.

The whole authenticity of this chapter of Matthew is less and less disputed nowadays by opponents of the Catholic faith. So it is that Professor Cullmann, the author of the work on St Peter to which I have already referred—and who, I repeat, is a Protestant—admits positively "that today the antiquity of this passage and its Palestinian origin are no longer in doubt". And he stresses that, "from a linguistic point of view, these verses have a wholly semitic character". On the subject of its semitic features Harnack wrote fifty years ago: "There are few texts in the Gospels, even longer ones, where the Aramaic origin shows itself so clearly in idea and expression as in this short passage." In fact, the designation of Peter Bar-Jona, the expression "flesh and blood", the terms "bind and loose", the "keys of the kingdom of heaven", the "gates of hell", the strophic rhythm—three strophes of three verses each—that one finds also in other words of Jesus, and, finally, the image of the rock-foundation, which has its equivalent in Rabbinic literature where Abraham is called "the rock of the world"—all this is profoundly and typically semitic.

Another argument also can be invoked. At the very moment when Simon appeared before Jesus for the first time, Jesus, as we have seen, said to him, wholly unexpectedly, "Thou art Simon the son of Jona; thou shalt be called Cephas." Jesus almost commanded him to take this name, and with such authority that the fisherman from Bethsaida had to accept, and answered ever afterwards to the name of Peter. Why should Jesus have chosen this symbolic name, why should he thus have baptized this new disciple, if he was not casting him for a fundamental rôle? Is it logical to suspect, because the verse from St Matthew is an inconvenient one, that it may have received an interpolation, and yet not to make any similar suggestion about the verse in St John's Gospel which foreshadows and explains it? The two texts are but part of a single whole.

In the second place, is it not clear that Peter receives from Jesus—as a promise, but of a conclusive kind—supreme authority within the Church that was to be founded after the Saviour had departed from this world? Our separated brethren admit the importance of this text, but they set themselves to diminish its implications. According to them, Peter was only appointed by Jesus to be a kind of official spokesman for the apostles. Did he not hold that position already? Is it not striking to find that Peter is *always mentioned first* in the Gospel narratives? That he always comes at the head of all the lists of the apostles? Does not St Matthew expressly say, "first, Simon, also called Peter" (10.2)? When St Mark describes the apostles looking for Jesus, does he not simply write, "Simon and his companions", as though taking it for granted that Simon Peter was the normal leader of that band? Is it not in the house of Simon Peter that Jesus comes to live in Capharnaum? Is it not nearly always Simon Peter who speaks when Jesus puts questions to his disciples? On the day of the resurrection, when Mary Magdalen, Mary the mother of James and Salome, having bought perfumes to embalm Jesus, arrive at the sepulchre, what is said to them by the young man wearing a white robe who is waiting for them? "No need to be dismayed; you have come to look for Jesus of Nazareth, who was crucified; he has risen again, he is not here. Here is the place where they laid him. Go and tell *Peter and the rest of his disciples* that he is going before you into Galilee. There you shall have sight of him, as he promised you" (Mark 16.6–7).

This is not all. Read again, with care, the words, "Thou art Peter and upon this rock I will build my church." Does this symbolic name, chosen, desired, imposed by Christ from the beginning of his public ministry, this prodigious pun, contain no delegation of authority, no plan? Can it be that a stone on which, as is solemnly declared, an edifice is to be built, is not what is called a foundation-stone—the essential foundation, the basis, the support upon which all is to rest? Is this a reference to a temporary, passing, limited work of building, as it were accidental, or to a definitive one? Can one take out

the first stone without placing the whole edifice in peril? Is
such a withdrawal even possible?

I know the Protestant thesis. Our separated brethren do not
dispute the special rôle of Peter among the disciples. They
even admit that the fisherman from Bethsaida was the "foundation". But there, according to them, his special position, his
privilege, his preeminence come to an end. First stone, yes;
corner-stone, it may be. But nothing more. Yet a "first stone",
a "corner-stone" on which nothing rested would be neither a
first stone nor a corner-stone; the adjectives demand that
something shall follow.

Let us go further. Christ does not content himself with saying
to Simon Peter, "Thou art Peter and upon this stone I will
build my church." He says also, "I will give to thee the keys
of the kingdom of heaven; and whatever thou shalt bind on
earth shall be bound in heaven; and whatever thou shalt loose
on earth shall be loosed in heaven." Did so imposing a mandate,
so extraordinary a natural and supernatural power, then confer
upon Simon Peter only the modest rôle of "spokesman for the
apostles" to which it is sought to reduce it? Are we to believe
that the simple fact of being "the first" among the disciples
was enough to give him the power to "bind and loose"?

No. If words have a meaning we are bound to recognize that
on that day in the year 29 Christ conferred exceptional authority
on one of his disciples. From which it follows that this prodigious privilege is not to be reconciled with the theory which
reduces Peter to the rank of "first" or simple "spokesman" of
the apostles.

The second text on which we base our faith comes in St
Luke's Gospel (22.31–2).

This time we are at the end of the historical life of our Lord.
It is the day of the Last Supper. Christ has just instituted the
Eucharist. He has pronounced the eternal words. There comes
a moment when he turns to Simon Peter and says to him:
"Simon, Simon, behold, Satan has claimed power over you all,
so that he can sift you like wheat: but I have prayed for thee,

that thy faith may not fail; when, after a while, thou hast come back to me, it is for thee to be the support of thy brethren."

This text, which has provoked no controversy, gives rise to very significant considerations. Jesus has his disciples about him, the last of the faithful, even the one who is to betray him; they are those who have remained with him to the very end of his life on earth. These disciples are to become the apostles. The creation, the development of the Church will be entrusted to them. Such is the future. And, for all this, the Saviour has no illusions. From all eternity he knows that these apostles, the support of his Church, are and will remain weak men. Simon Peter will deny him tomorrow, in the hour of danger. Jesus predicts this to him almost at once. But nevertheless this fisherman—in all senses of the word—will remain "the Man-Rock". And it is to him that at the Last Supper Jesus turns for "the support of his brethren". Once again he is entrusted with the confidence of the Son of God.

Finally, the unique powers conferred upon Peter find striking confirmation in a text from St John's Gospel, the last chapter of which describes a second miraculous draught of fishes obtained, at the command of Jesus, in the sea of Tiberias, after the resurrection:

> And when they had eaten, Jesus said to Simon Peter, Simon, son of John, dost thou care for me more than these others? Yes, Lord, he told him, thou knowest well that I love thee. And he said to him, Feed my lambs. And again, a second time, he asked him, Simon, son of John, dost thou care for me? Yes, Lord, he told him, thou knowest well that I love thee. He said to him, Tend my shearlings. Then he asked him a third question, Simon, son of John, dost thou love me? Peter was deeply moved when he was asked a third time, Dost thou love me? and said to him, Lord, thou knowest all things; thou canst tell that I love thee. Jesus said to him, Feed my sheep (John 21.15–17).

Thus does Jesus insistently question Simon Peter about the love which he bears for him, as though he wanted so to test that devotion as to make him realize all the more keenly the importance of the commission which is being given to him. Three times, similarly, does Jesus repeat to him the mandate which he is entrusting to him: Feed my lambs. Even if one joins the majority of the commentators—if not all—in admitting that this threefold question of Christ's represents a sort of reminder of the threefold denial, and an opportunity offered to Peter to atone for it, a connection has unquestionably been established by Jesus between the necessity of love and the function of a shepherd of sheep. So speaks he who has placed charity above all else and for whom the love of God is the first of the commandments.

Professor Cullmann, who attributes this chapter to a different author than the rest of the fourth Gospel, is of the opinion that we must regard it as an addition that remains exactly in the line of what has gone before:

> In ending on this dialogue [he writes] the author of the twenty-first chapter makes it the crowning passage of the whole Gospel; this member of the Johannine circle, whose identity remains a mystery, shows in this way how he interprets the work as a whole. In doing this he undoubtedly puts the emphasis too strongly on one of the intentions of the Fourth Gospel. But in bringing the two disciples face to face and showing how each receives from the Risen Christ, each in his own way, a special task, he shows that he has understood the plan of his predecessor: Peter is placed in the position of a shepherd.[2]

Summing up what he has said about the four Gospels, Professor Cullmann concludes: "The whole tradition of the Gospels testifies that Peter occupies an especially representative position among the disciples of Jesus." So long as Jesus lives that position will not be that of head, but after the death of Christ it is certainly to Peter that the flock, both lambs and sheep, is entrusted.

And this pastoral responsibility is clearly that of governing the Church which is to be born.

So a series of events and incidents join to confer on Simon Peter, during the historical life of Jesus and after his resurrec-

[2] *Op. cit.,* p. 24.

tion, a place apart in the group of the disciples who are to become the apostles and the founders of the Church. From these events, from these incidents, we infer "the primacy of Peter". Moreover, that primacy is, we may say, no longer disputed by one school of Protestants at least. But while we Catholics infer from these texts the right to confer on Peter a kind of magisterium, from the time when Christ leaves this earth, and while we maintain the privilege of that magisterium in the Church of Rome which he founded and in the popes who have succeeded him at the head of that Church, our Protestant brethren no longer follow us in this logical development. For them the mission of Peter was limited in time. It did not amount to any exceptional privilege for him. In any case, it came to an end with Peter's departure from Jerusalem. It was not open to a succession. We Catholics on the other hand consider that the papacy is its legitimate outcome. The Protestants deny not only that legitimacy but the logic of that outcome.

Here, then, we are at the heart of the problem which divides us. I propose to enumerate the principal reasons on which our conviction rests. I shall analyse and illustrate the principal arguments of those who raise objections against us. I shall endeavour to show conclusively why, taking these objections into account, our certainty remains complete.

To know what happened after Christ's ascension into heaven we must read the Acts of the Apostles, and must treat that narrative, as we have done with the Gospels, both as an historical document and as a sacred and inspired text.

The Acts of the Apostles is as explicit as possible. Listen again to Professor Cullmann:

"In reading the book of the Acts", he writes, "one notices that, without any possible doubt, Peter occupies a special place in the first Church, which was that of Jerusalem."[3] "Whatever may be his exact powers", he writes again, very prudently, "he presides . . ."

In the first part of the Acts of the Apostles we find, indeed,

[3] *Op. cit.*, p. 29.

numerous references to the special rôle which St Peter plays in the beginnings of the Church. We quote Fr Yves de la Brière, who has collected them:

> Between the Ascension and Pentecost, it is Peter who presides when Matthias is chosen to complete the college of twelve, replacing the traitor Judas (1.15–26). On the day of Pentecost, it is Peter who is the spokesman, and who acts as the leader of the Christian community: the text indeed distinguishes, "Peter with the eleven" (2.14); "Peter and his fellow Apostles" (37). We find the same role for Peter at the time of the healing of the lame man at the gate of the temple, and the preaching to the people and the new extension of the new-born Church which follows from that event (3.1–26; 4.4–6). It is Peter who, arraigned with John before the Jewish Sanhedrin, testifies officially, in the name of the whole community of the disciples of Jesus (4.5–22). It is Peter who acts as the minister of God and chief pastor of the Church of Christ in the punishment of Ananias and Sapphira (5.1–11). It is Peter who appears a second time before the Sanhedrin and speaks in the name of all the young Christian body. Luke, the chronicler, uses the words "Peter and the other Apostles" (5.29) to describe the group. Peter, with John, goes into Samaria to lay hands on the converts who have been baptized by the deacon Philip, and it is Peter who utters a terrible warning to Simon Magus (8.14–24). Peter works remarkable miracles while he is going from town to town visiting the Christian churches (11.31–43). When Peter is imprisoned by order of King Herod Agrippa, and is shortly to be miraculously delivered, the whole Church prays for the liberation of the supreme pastor which, when it takes place, causes immense joy among the faithful (12.3–17). Finally, the part played by Peter in the conciliar assembly of the pastors of the Church at Jerusalem can reasonably be regarded as that of the president of the assembly (15.6–12). From this collection of facts the primacy of Peter, based on the institution of Christ, appears as it was being exercised and acted upon. The new-born Church possesses a visible head, and that head is Peter, the Prince of the apostles.[4]

There is nothing to suggest that this authority, which is

[4] Yves de la Brière, *Dictionnaire Apologétique de la Foi Catholique*, part 17 (1921).

recognized in Peter, is limited to the town of Jerusalem. It is exercised no less actively in Samaria, in Lydda, in Joppa, in Caesarea. It is in this last town that Peter wins for the Church of Christ the centurion Cornelius, the first convert from paganism, with all his household. And when the Herodian persecution obliges him, after his miraculous deliverance from prison, to leave Jerusalem and to go "elsewhere"—according to the mysterious word of the Acts (12.17)—it is evident that he relinquishes nothing of the title and the powers which he has received from Christ. Peter does not change his name, and his name does not change its meaning. He is and he remains "the Rock". So will he be wherever he goes. Whether he is at Antioch, Pontus, Galatia, Cappadocia or Bithynia, places where he stayed, as we know from his first Epistle; whether he is—at least in travelling—after this date of the year 42 at Rome, or elsewhere, everywhere he goes he remains the leader, the shepherd of the lambs and of the sheep. The name of Peter, which means the foundation, has become inseparable from his person. He carries and takes about with him his position as a Rock. And as that position is one of those which can never again be absent from the Church, any more than the foundation of a building can be taken away, all the indications are that the successors of Peter must inherit his titles, his mission, his authority. The whole doctrine of the Catholic Church rests upon this basis.

Let us rapidly mention some among the proofs we possess of the continuity of the powers exercised by Peter even after his departure from Jerusalem.

When Paul is chosen by the Holy Spirit to be the apostle of the Gentiles, he feels, as he tells in the Epistle to the Galatians, the need to have his mission approved by the heads of the Church of Jerusalem. Peter has left Jerusalem for the first time, but has returned there for a short while. It is to him that Paul addresses himself in the first place. He comes "to visit Peter". It is from him that he seeks as it were a confirmation of the divine call which he has received. Later on, when Paul submits the first results of his apostolate to that assembly which is commonly called the Council of Jerusalem, it is Peter who speaks first; and he decides eventually in favour of Paul, despite the opposition of the Jewish Christians. All the company are then won over to his view by the voice of James.

Mgr Charles Journet, in his study of the primacy of Peter according to Protestant and Catholic teaching, brings out clearly that the apostolate was "substantially the same in all the apostles"; all could bear witness to the resurrection of Jesus, reveal Christian truth and write canonical books and, so far as jurisdiction is concerned, could undertake missions, found local Churches and incorporate them within the universal Church. But Peter had received in addition a unique privilege which on this third point—that of jurisdiction—places him from the first above all the apostles. Thus Mgr Journet emphasizes the distinction between the apostles as apostles and the apostles as "sheep of Christ", deprived of the visible presence since the ascension and entrusted by him to the care of Peter, the one shepherd. So the apostles, as St Paul calls them, are "the legates of Christ to carry on Christ's plan, to found local Churches, to incorporate them in the universal Church; Peter alone is the *Vicar* of Christ, the supreme recipient of jurisdiction".

Those of our separated brethren who are least removed from our ideas admit, as I have said, the special rôle given by the Master to Simon Peter. Certainly they limit it in time. In their eyes Peter is only distinguished from the other apostles by a sort of "chronological precedence", and that for a determined and relatively brief period. The Rock-Apostle was only once at the head of the universal Church, in the days which followed the resurrection of Christ and in those which saw the coming of the Holy Spirit, a time when he presided over the Mother Church of Jerusalem and exercised there the power of binding and loosing as the story of Ananias and Sapphira remains to show. "Peter retains nonetheless for all centuries", writes Professor Cullmann, "the incomparable splendour and honour of having been, in the first days of the Church of Jesus Christ, the head of the first community—that is, of what was then the whole Church. This is a fact which belongs to the history of salvation."

In order thus to limit the supreme mission of Peter to a brief period at the dawn of the Church, Protestantism—and I mean the Protestant school which recognizes the temporary pre-eminence of Peter—bases its arguments on four principal contentions:

1. The apostles had clearly received equal powers from Jesus, including that of binding and loosing. There was, then, equality between them. From this follows the impossibility of establishing a sort of "succession" to a "supreme power" which did not in fact exist.

2. That this was the position is proved by the replacement of the apostle Peter by the apostle James as head of the Church of Jerusalem, only a little while after the departure of Jesus from the earth. Peter, therefore, did not regard himself as the holder of a "supreme power", since he yielded the position to James.

3. The principle of the authority of Peter over the other apostles is inconsistent with the fact that heated discussions—one might almost go so far as to speak of a conflict—divided Peter and Paul over the Antiochene issue.

4. Basing themselves on this last incident, some Protestants go so far as to conclude that schism was established in the heart of the Church from the very beginning of Christianity—an opinion which, let it be said in passing, sets in a curious light the second fundamental text which establishes the authority of Peter over the apostles; I refer to Luke 22.31-2. Did not Jesus indeed know that disagreements were to appear among his disciples, and did he not anticipate the risk of disintegration, and so of schism, by the imperative words, "be the support of thy brethren"?

But let us briefly examine the Protestant arguments as I have set them forth.

It is beyond dispute that in the same Gospel where St Matthew records, in the sixteenth chapter, the *Tu es Petrus* and

the powers of binding and loosing, we are told, a little further
on, in the eighteenth chapter, that Jesus, addressing no longer
Simon Peter alone but his disciples, spoke thus: "I promise
you, all that you bind on earth shall be bound in heaven, and
all that you loose on earth shall be loosed in heaven" (18.18).
So far is the Catholic Church from being unaware of this
second text, so far is she from underestimating its significance,
that it is upon this very passage that she bases the power of
bishops. According to Catholic doctrine, bishops are indeed
the successors of the apostles, and each bishop, from this fact,
possesses the right to bind and to loose. Does it follow that the
power recognized in Peter alone in the earlier chapter loses its
meaning from the fact that later on it is also attributed to his
companions? By no means. Turn from the principles to the
facts: the existence of bishops, the powers of which every
bishop disposes within his own jurisdiction, in no way detract
from or weaken those which belong exclusively to the pope.
To argue in the opposite sense would oblige us to hold that
Jesus must have reserved for one single man *all* jurisdiction
within the Church that was to be created, which would have
been to make that task quite impossible and to contradict the
missionary action of the new-born Church, the clear command
to "go out, making disciples of all nations". But it is enough
to read Matthew 16.17–19 closely and as a whole: the words,
"whatever thou shalt bind and whatever thou shalt loose",
follow "and I will give to thee the keys of the kingdom of
heaven"—which, especially in the language of the time, represents the granting of something like the position of a viceroy.
But when Jesus is addressing all the apostles together he no
longer speaks of the keys of the kingdom of heaven. We can
only conclude from these texts that Simon Peter has the same
jurisdiction as his fellow disciples for the administration of
the sacraments of the Church, but that to Simon Peter alone
the Lord has transmitted powers of a general order. And this
precisely represents the dispositions of the hierarchy of the
Catholic, Apostolic and Roman Church. One can say that that
hierarchy is modelled on what we read in the sixteenth and
eighteenth chapters of Matthew.

So I come to the second Protestant objection, about the replacement of Peter by James at the head of the Church of Jerusalem. The answer here is clear. If Peter yielded the government of the Church of Jerusalem to James, it was in order to dedicate himself exclusively to his missionary activity; it was to obey the Master's first commandment, to "go out, making disciples". One can in no way compare the arrangements of the infant Church to those of our own times, or even to those of the centuries which have intervened. Jerusalem could not become the centre of the Church; it was neither at the centre of the future Christendom nor easily reached from the Christian communities which were springing up. Peter could leave Jerusalem and its Church, could entrust them to James, without thereby abandoning the mission which the Master had given him; it was, indeed, to keep faithful to that mission that he left Jerusalem. And so true is this that, after visiting parts of Asia Minor, what does Peter do? He leaves for Rome, the capital of the Roman world, the centre towards which all attention is turned, from which, directly or indirectly, everything derives. It is there that he founded the Church to which, as we shall shortly see, all the other Churches conformed.

The discussions which brought St Peter and St Paul into opposition have been given in history the name of "the Antiochene dispute". Antioch had become a much more important Christian centre than Jerusalem, and it was, indeed, at Antioch that the name of Christian first appeared (which shows, moreover, that the Church of Jerusalem did not possess, or possessed no longer, the supremacy which some have tried to attribute to it in order to maintain a certain thesis). It is beyond doubt that between Peter and Paul there was, not a divergence of doctrine or teaching, but a divergence of attitude towards the new converts. Peter made use of Mosaic observances; Paul wanted to free his followers from them. But if Paul defended his ideas before Peter in a vigorous manner, it was because he recognized the special authority which Peter possessed. He knew that the future of the Church could depend upon his attitude. Barnabas had already adopted Peter's view.

If Paul had not possessed so profound a "sense of the Church" —that is, of the *necessary* unity of the Church—he would have appealed to God against Peter. Those who are not afraid of heresy always do something of that kind. But no, Paul appeals to Peter hesitant, to Peter changing, to Peter submitting to the doctrine adopted at the Council of Jerusalem. "I resisted him to his face," says the apostle of the Gentiles.

This was not a matter of doctrinal conflict. But in the attitude of Peter towards the ancient practices of the Mosaic law lay a danger of supporting an error of principle. Paul wanted at all costs to lead Peter back to the logic of his own thought. He wanted at all costs to remain in agreement with him. The way he behaved proves Paul's courage and independence of mind. But it does not prove that Peter no longer had authority; quite the contrary. Nor does it prove the existence of anything like a state of schism, for it is precisely in order to avoid any possibility of dissension that the accounting between the two apostles was brusque. Their unity of view comes out of it strengthened. To speak of "schism" in the Church at the time when that Church is forming herself would amount to saying of an oak tree towering over a forest that it had been split since it was a sapling. Schism there was in the eleventh century; schism there was in the sixteenth; and those two schisms, alas, still persist. But in the first centuries of the life of the Christian Church, despite the countless heresies which did not cease to multiply from its first appearance (for men are men), the Church kept her unity. And that, indeed, is one of the most striking indications of her essentially supernatural character.

CHAPTER II

PETER AND THE CHURCH OF ROME

We now follow Peter to Rome. The foundation of a Christian community in the capital of the Roman world by the first of the apostles, his martyrdom and burial in Rome, are the crucial events on which the origins of the papacy are founded.

To understand these events we must consider three separate pieces of evidence: the language used by St Paul in his Epistle to the Romans, the written evidence of the primitive Church and the results of the recent excavations beneath the altar of the Confession in St Peter's at Rome.

Perhaps it may seem surprising that we confidently appeal in the first place to St Paul's Epistle to the Romans, for Peter is not mentioned therein by name, which shows that he was not in Rome when the Epistle was written. Many critics, indeed, have regarded St Paul's silence about him as an argument against the view that he ever went to Rome. Nicolas Corte has replied effectively to these critics: "It is impossible", he writes, "to read the stately Epistle to the Romans without being struck by the solemn manner in which it is written."[1] St Paul by no means regards the Romans as people unaware of the mysteries of the Christian religion. He does not confine himself to offering them, as he says, "milk" as nourishment, as one gives it to children. He embarks with them upon the fundamental problems, the most profound conceptions, of the new religion—the original fall; the consequences of Adam's

[1] *Saint Pierre est-il au Vatican?*

disobedience; the universal fall of men; the necessity of faith in Jesus Christ, the unique Redeemer of mankind; the efficacy of Christ's death; the meaning of his baptism; the divine paternity restored in him; the pouring forth of the Holy Spirit among men. "Paul thus regards the Romans as accomplished theologians." They must, therefore, already have been instructed; he has, so to speak, only to explain these matters more clearly to them, only to recall implicitly the agreement about them already established between Peter and himself.

It is quite true that he does not mention Peter by name. But there is no need for him to do so. The essential subject of this Epistle is precisely that with which the discussions of the Council of Jerusalem, and the differences which arose between Peter and himself at Antioch, had been concerned. However, if Paul does not mention Peter by name, he refers to him explicitly enough in explaining why he himself, having already travelled so far to announce the Christ, has not yet been to Rome, despite his desire to do so: "My own work has been to complete the preaching of Christ's Gospel, in a wide sweep from Jerusalem as far as Illyricum. It has been a point of honour with me to preach the Gospel thus, never in places where Christ's name was already known; *I would not build on the foundation another man had laid.*" And he concludes: "This was the chief reason which prevented me from visiting you." (Rom. 15.19–22.)

"Another man", then, had already been to Rome. And this "other man" had laid "the foundation". Observe that Paul does not say vaguely "the foundation other people had laid"; he is speaking explicitly of *one* other man. Now, apart from Peter, no other apostle has ever been associated with the foundation in Rome. So it follows that Paul can only have been thinking about Peter. What is more, the whole of his Epistle suggests this. When at the end of it, according to his custom, he sends "greetings", those whom he names, excellent Christians though they may be or may soon become, are, from all the evidence, only disciples. None of them has the stature of the head or founder of a Church. And, moreover, Paul knows

that the Romans are by no means lacking in Christian instruc-
tion, for he says to them exactly what he said to his own faithful of Corinth: "Brethren, I entreat you to keep a watch on
those who are causing dissension and doing hurt to consciences,
without regard to *the teaching which has been given you*"
(16.17). A German scholar, Mgr Holzner, writes in his admir-
able book on St Paul: "The position is, then, that Paul decides
to move the centre of gravity of his activity westwards. Rome,
the ruling city of the world, inspires him with the grand conception of a worldwide Church, universal and Catholic. One
thought only restrains him: true to his principles, he would
avoid building on foundations laid by someone else. He knows
that an apostolic personage has already laid the foundations
of Christianity in Rome. This can only mean Peter."

So the very clear impression emerges from the Epistle to the
Romans that the Church of Rome has had a founder, and that
that founder was a man of such authority that he, Paul, has not
thought it necessary to appear before that Church; that it has
been so well instructed as to be capable of understanding and
discussing the loftiest problems of the new doctrine; and,
finally, that the faithful of this Church must not be among
those who are "without regard to the teaching given". If all
this preparation of the Roman Church is not the work of Peter,
to whom can it be attributed? No name can be brought forward. We do not know of any other apostle who could be
connected with so momentous a foundation. This title of
founder has always been reserved for Peter alone.

Now, since the texts which we shall shortly cite all point
only to Peter, it must be agreed that *before the year 58*—the
date commonly assigned to the Epistle to the Romans—Peter
had already been to Rome, and that he had already laid there
the foundations of the Church. Otherwise the scruples of St
Paul would have no point.

It must have taken time to lay those foundations. Even if
it is not admitted that Peter went to Rome as early as the year
42, it is certain that in 51 or 52 there were such disturbances
among the Jews of Rome over a certain Chrestus, as the pagan

historian Suetonius calls him, that the Emperor Claudius, who was by no means an enemy of Jews, felt obliged to expel them from the city. Among those expelled were Aquilas and his wife Priscilla, whom Paul met at Corinth. It was by them—and this is certain—that he was so fully informed about what was being said and done among the Christians of Rome. Perhaps they were the leaders of that group whose members said at Corinth, "I am for Cephas" (1 Cor. 1.12).

It will be readily agreed, therefore, that the violent "troubles" which had disturbed the Jewish community in Rome had their origin in the preaching of the Gospel of Christ, and that those responsible for that preaching were Peter and the group of disciples who followed him everywhere he went.

Support for this is to be found in an impressive collection of written evidence bearing on St Peter's arrival in Rome, of which we can do no more than mention the principal examples.

In the first place there are the two Epistles of St Peter. In the first of these Peter refers to himself by name at the very beginning and at the end indicates the place from which he is writing with these mysterious words: "The Church here in Babylon, united with you by God's election, sends you her greeting; so does my son, Mark." (1 Peter 5.13.) Most of the commentators, as is well known, think that "Babylon" can only mean Rome. Professor Cullmann says without reservation, "The interpretation which sees in Babylon a conventional name for Rome seems to us by far the most likely."[2] Mgr Duchesne, who was very careful about studying and drawing conclusions from texts, is still more positive: "The fact is", he says, "that St Peter himself does not fail to document his presence in Rome. His letter to the Christians of Asia Minor ends with a greeting which he sends them in the name of the Church of Babylon; that is, of the Church of Rome. This symbolism is very well known, if only from the Apocalypse" (cf. Apoc. 17.5).

[2] *Op. cit.*, p. 72.

The coming of St Peter to Rome is clearly attested, in the second place, by the Epistle of St Clement to the Corinthians, which dates from the year 96. This very important letter, which we shall have to discuss later on, speaks *incidentally*—which is more significant than would be a statement deliberately intended—of SS. Peter and Paul. It calls them "our excellent apostles". It commemorates their martyrdom, and places it in Rome. Yet the notion that Peter and Paul might have governed the Church of Rome together has never been put forward. Peter alone was the head of that Church, even when Paul was there at the same time as he.

Ten or twelve years after Clement's letter from Rome, the Bishop of Antioch, Ignatius, addresses the Romans, to beg them not to cheat him of the happiness of dying for Christ: and he says to them: "I do not give you orders, as did Peter and Paul. They were apostles, and I am only a man under sentence." He in his turn associates in Rome the two names of Peter and Paul. Speaking of Ignatius, Professor Cullmann writes: "Did such a linking of Peter and Paul follow as a matter of course when a man was thinking of apostolic names? At a later time perhaps, but not by any means in the time of Ignatius."

After Ignatius of Antioch the evidence becomes increasingly abundant. The most important items in it include the letter of Bishop Dionysius of Corinth, towards the year 170; the testimony of St Irenaeus in his *Adversus Haereses*, to which we shall return later; and the statements of Tertullian about the year 200 and then towards 216 or 217.

After that time the fact that the Church of Rome had been founded by Peter is something well established in the Christian world. But the name of Peter is inseparable from the name of Paul. If there had once been differences between them at Antioch, they are indeed forgotten. Peter and Paul have become the glory of the Church of Rome. On June 29th the Church honours them both in the same feast.

About the year 200, the priest Gaius, wishing to refute a certain Proclus, of the Montanist sect, could write to him:

"And for myself, I can display nothing less than the trophies of the apostles, for if you go to the Vatican or along the road to Ostia you will find there the trophies of the founders of this Church."

And so we come to the new proof provided by the results of the excavations recently carried out beneath the basilica of St Peter in Rome.

Here again we shall confine ourselves to noting what is essential, referring the reader to the specialized works on this absorbing question.[3] The excavations at St Peter's have led to conclusions that were wholly unforeseen and are of capital importance. Carried out at the order of Pius XII between 1940 and 1949, the results obtained have been comprehensively set forth in a two-volume work entitled *Esplorazioni sotto la Confessione di San Pietro.*

The weightiest argument for the presence of St Peter's tomb at the Vatican at the time when Constantine's basilica was built is the fact that it was built on such an extremely inconvenient site. The ground sloped so steeply as to make very great preliminary excavations necessary. Yet quite close by the ground was level. Now under the altar of the Confession in Constantine's basilica, at a depth of exactly seven metres, directly beneath, measured with a plumb-line (the altar of the Confession in the present basilica is ten metres higher), there is a tomb. It is clear, then, that the tomb must have been a famous one, providing a compelling reason for Constantine to choose this place, despite the lie of the land, as the site of the basilica.

Another consideration also shows that this site was regarded as a sacred one. All round the tomb a cemetery, both pagan and Christian, has been discovered, in which most of the tombs go back to the second and third centuries, and some to the first century, about the year 70. Now the Emperor Constantine

[3] See the Select Bibliography at the end of this volume.

did not scruple to destroy part of this cemetery in order to build his church. For that purpose he not merely sacrificed works of art; he violated the most respected of the traditions of Rome, which forbade anyone to disturb the sleep of the dead. Mausoleums belonging to some of the most powerful Roman families—the Marcii, the Mattuccii, the Popilii, the Tullii, the Valerii, and so on—were treated without any consideration. It is certain, then, that he must have had very important reasons for building his basilica in this place, since he had both to overcome the great difficulties presented by the lie of the land and to violate what was something like a sacred law. How, then, in view of this, can we doubt that the altar of the Confession was built above the founder of the Church?

Professor Cullmann, in a book which is both honest and comprehensive, admits the force of these arguments. He himself considers that this place is, if I may put it so, full of St Peter. But he is not led to believe in the existence of the tomb. He inclines rather towards the theory of a "trophy"—the trophy of Gaius—which would have marked the very spot of the sufferings of the first apostle. "We must admit", he writes, "that there was *a special reason* [Professor Cullmann's italics] for building it [Constantine's basilica] exactly on the steep slope. That reason can only be the following: the place which Constantine's contemporaries regarded as the site of the execution or the burial of Peter was not simply the region of the Vatican Hill; it was this particular slope, and even, it seems, a precise point on this slope."

Dare I add that the distinction between the tomb and the actual place of suffering does not seem to me of great importance? No one has ever claimed that the bones of Peter have been discovered in this tomb. It is known that the relics were taken to the catacombs at the time of the persecution of 258. Whether the site on which were built both the altar of the Confession of Constantine's basilica and the altar of the Confession of the basilica of Paul V may be that where the mortal remains of the apostle were entombed or where the apostle suffered martyrdom, the significance is the same, the veneration is the same, the proof is the same. It is certainly there, in either case, that the Church of Rome—that is, the Universal Church—possesses her greatest memorial and her first foundation.

CHAPTER III

ST PETER'S SUCCESSORS

To understand how the primacy of Peter came to be handed on to the popes, we must try to understand the setting of the Church's earliest development. Our minds are so made that we nearly always reason in terms of the setting in which we live, and, *a fortiori*, of the time to which we belong. To gain even a very approximate idea of the beginnings of the Church, one must have some notion of the world in which that Church appeared and the conditions under which she was formed, as they were at that time. "It would be as foolish", writes Abbé Mourret in his book on the papacy, "to imagine the first pope carried on a sort of *sedia gestatoria* with the *flabelli* waving about him as it would be to imagine the first of the Merovingian Kings seated on a throne with the courtiers and the ceremonies of the Court of Louis XIV." The comparison is a good one. The papacy was to develop little by little; was to assume its procedures, its form, its plenitude, little by little. But the seed from which it sprang and the stem which grew from that seed were well defined and without blemishes.

The first age of the Church can be described as the apostolic age. It is characterized by a good deal of fluidity in its conditions, inasmuch as, on the one hand, the apostles were not attached to fixed sees, but exercised their authority wherever they went and, on the other hand, all the writings of the apostles came to be regarded as inspired by God and therefore became part of the canon of Scripture. It is because of these two characteristics that some people, Professor Cullmann among them, say that the powers of the apostles were not transmissible.

After the apostolic age the leaders of the Church had each a definite station, and their writings were no longer admitted to the canon of Scripture. The deposit of revelation closed with the death of St John, the last of the apostles. The fluid period nevertheless ended in stability. Bishops everywhere succeeded the apostles; and by the same reasoning we say that the popes succeeded Peter. We derive this conclusion not from biblical texts but from the facts themselves.

Here I should like to say something in parenthesis, in order to indicate briefly one of the essential differences between the Catholic and Protestant conceptions of the history of Christianity.

Our separated brethren start from the principle that the Scriptures alone are the source alike of all truth and all authority within the Church. In our view this unqualified "biblicism" goes beyond the Bible. Nowhere in the Bible is it said that the Bible is the sole means chosen by Jesus Christ for the transmission of his truth and his authority. Unqualified biblicism is not biblical.

Jesus Christ wrote nothing; nor did he command anyone to write. He did not choose the Scriptures as the vehicle of the deposit of revelation. In regard to the powers of Peter, in particular, it is evident that they were not based on Scripture for the very good reason that the basic texts which we have already quoted, which many Protestants agree in regarding as proof of Peter's preeminence, *are nevertheless antedated by the exercise of that preeminence.* Who would dare to maintain that Christ did not found a Church that was intended in his mind to endure through the centuries? Can it be maintained, therefore, that recourse to the Bible was enough to maintain unity within that Church, both in its difficult beginnings and in the time that followed; that the powers entrusted by Jesus to Peter in the apostolic college concerned only that disciple, and that college; that they were not meant to be transmitted after their death?

It is our faith in the divinity of Christ which is at the root of our faith in the everlasting nature of the Church and of her unitary constitution. And that constitution is only truly *unitary* if we admit, within the Church, a sovereign authority, under the guidance of the Holy Spirit. That sovereign authority is the papacy.

Such is what could have been said *a priori*, starting only from the divinity of Christ and from the desire for unity which he had expressed in these words, in the supreme prayer at the Last Supper: "Holy Father, keep them true to thy name . . . that they may be one, as we are one. . . . It is not only for them that I pray; I pray for those who are to find faith in me through their word; that they may all be one; that they too may be one in us, as thou, Father, art in me, and I in thee; so that the world may come to believe that it is thou who hast sent me" (John 17.11,20). For Catholics, the continuance of the hierarchy within the structure of the new-born Church is not only an act of faith; not only a deduction made by reason, in the field of fact as in the field of psychology; it is likewise confirmed by the sequence of events and evidence.

The transition from the itinerant apostolate to the residential episcopate was general in the Church. It was spontaneously effected, a natural development, coming about as a matter of course, without any danger to the new-found unity among Christians. The first Christians did not ask themselves the questions which were to be so much discussed later on. The first difficulties appeared very much later, and when the decisive phase was already over. Then, and then only, did the Church make use of episcopal registers and written texts that were thereafter received as canonical.

In order that no contention should arise against their juridical power, the bishops identified themselves with the apostles

who had preceded and instituted them. In the year 96, St
Clement of Rome, in his Epistle to the Corinthians, defines in
these terms the method by which the power of God was transmitted to Christ, from Christ to the apostles, and from the
apostles to the bishops:

> The apostles for our sakes received the Gospel from the Lord
> Jesus Christ; Jesus Christ was sent from God. Christ then is
> from God, and the apostles from Christ. . . . And so, as they
> preached in the country and in the towns, they appointed their
> first fruits (having proved them by the Spirit) to be bishops and
> deacons of them that should believe. . . . Our apostles knew also,
> through our Lord Jesus Christ, that there would be strife over
> the dignity of the bishop's office. For this reason therefore,
> having received complete foreknowledge, they appointed the
> aforesaid, and after a time made provision that on their death
> other approved men should succeed to their ministry. And in
> this manner were installed by them, or, in the times which
> followed, by other excellent men, with the consent of the whole
> Church, those who have blamelessly served Christ's flock in
> humility, peace and generosity.[1]

Now what happened "in the whole Church" happened above
all at Rome. St Clement, the author of these lines, is himself
the witness to it: he was the third successor of St Peter. We
shall shortly see what kind of authority he exercised *outside*
Rome.

The care that was taken to justify the episcopal authority,
as we have just seen it shown in the words of St Clement in the
year 96, is shown by the care with which the episcopal lists
were kept up to date. For the succession of Peter no hesitation
was shown. The earliest individual whom we find giving his
attention to the register of the popes is Hegesippus, a Palestine
Jew who was converted to Christianity. He travelled round the
Churches to contrast their unity with the variety of the heretics

[1] Clement, *ad Corinth.*, xlii, xliv. The translation of all save the last
sentence is that given by Henry Bettenson, *Documents of the Christian
Church*; Oxford University Press: World's Classics.

—already!—and visited in particular those of Corinth and Rome, about the years 155 to 166. He died about 180. Eusebius of Caesarea, who possessed the writings of Hegesippus, quotes this passage from them:

"When I came to Rome, I made for myself a succession-list as far as Anicetus; whose deacon was Eleutherius. Soter succeeded Anicetus, after him Eleutherius. In every succession, and in every city, things are as the law and the prophets and the Lord preach."[2]

It is perhaps from Hegesippus that St Irenaeus borrowed the list which he gives in the following text:

The blessed apostles [Peter and Paul], after founding and building up the Church [of Rome], entrusted the office of bishop to Linus. Paul speaks of this Linus in his epistles to Timothy. Anacletus followed him. After him, in the third place after the apostles, Clement was appointed bishop. . . . Evaristus succeeded this Clement, and Alexander Evaristus, and then Sixtus, the sixth after the apostles, was appointed. After him came Telesphorus, who had a glorious martyrdom. Then came Hyginus, Pius, Anicetus, Soter and Eleutherius, the twelfth from the apostles who now occupies the see.[3]

An exactly similar list may be found in the book *Against the Heresies*, written by St Epiphanius, Bishop of Constantia-Salamis, on the island of Cyprus, between the years 367 and 403.

But what is important to notice is that in the whole of this no recourse to the Bible is to be found. It was not the fundamental texts which we quoted and discussed in the preceding chapter that established the papacy. It was the authority of Christ, of which these texts are a written attestation, but not the chief one. If episcopal lists are drawn up, it is not in the least in a spirit of historical documentation. It is nothing like the compilation of orderly archives. We have heard Clement of Rome give us this rule: God sent Christ, Christ sent the

[2] Translation in *Documents Illustrating Papal Authority*, ed. Giles (S.P.C.K., 1952).

[3] Translation *loc. cit.*; the names being here Latinized according to the usual convention.

apostles, the apostles established the bishops. The right passes by that unbroken chain. All that Peter was in the college of the apostles and in the primitive Church, the Bishop of Rome, his successor, is and must be in the Church of his time. Appeal was to be made to the biblical texts in the theoretical discussions of a later day. But at first there was no question of doing so.

Let us try to understand from the conditions of the first centuries how the powers assumed by the successors of Peter and recognized by the rest of the Church were exercised. The "grain of mustard-seed" had only just left the earth; it was far from becoming "taller than any garden herb". The most important surviving evidence regarding the papal authority is the letter to the Corinthians of Pope Clement of Rome, dating from 96 or 98, the testimony of St Ignatius of Antioch, of Hegesippus and of Dionysius of Corinth, the papal interventions in the discussions about the date of Easter, the attestations of St Irenaeus, the authority assumed by St Callistus and rejected by Tertullian, the attitude of St Cyprian towards the popes of his time, the affair of the two Dionysiuses at the end of the third century.

First, the letter of Pope Clement, which is generally believed to be almost certainly older than the Fourth Gospel. Professor Cullmann places it, "at least from a chronological point of view, in the setting of the New Testament". St John, the last survivor of the apostles, was still living, amid universal veneration. The occasion of this letter was as follows. Dissensions had arisen within the Church of Corinth, the most important of the communities in Greece. To settle them it should have been possible to turn to John who, living at Ephesus, was relatively near. John had known Christ. He was the only survivor of the twelve apostles. Who could have greater authority and prestige? However, the fact is that it was Clement, the Bishop of Rome, who intervened, whether on his own initiative, which would have implied a remarkable awareness of his authority, or whether at the request of the clergy of Corinth against whom the dissensions were directed, which would show what authority the Bishop of Rome enjoyed in the eyes of those clergy. From beginning to end Clement's letter breathes moderation and calm. He speaks in the name of all his Church. He commands nothing, but he gives very strong advice. He proposes three principles of solution. He reminds everyone, as we have already said, of the chain of transmission: God, Christ, the apostles, the bishops. That sequence is enough to show what obedience is due to a bishop. At Corinth this must not be forgotten.

But what shows that Clement does not intend to confine himself to addressing a verbal exhortation to the Church of Corinth is that he sends it envoys charged to act as arbiters. Would he have been able to do this without the previous assent of the clergy to whose assistance he was going? It is more than probable that his intervention was requested. The rest matters little. That solemn intervention shows clearly that the thought of Clement is not animated only by a desire for fraternal charity towards a neighbouring community which is disturbed. *His language is a recall to order. He intends to make it apply to Corinth.* Doubtless he disposed of no other weapons than those of persuasion, of no other sanctions than those which strike the sin of disobedience. Nevertheless he does not hesitate to emphasize the gravity of that sin. His conclusion above all is worth noting:

> Receive our counsel, and you will have no cause to regret. . . . But if any disobey the words spoken by him [God] through us, let them know that they will involve themselves in transgression and no small danger. But we shall be innocent of this sin. . . . It is right, then, that, confronted by so many examples, we should bow the neck and take the seat of obedience. . . . For you will give us joy and gladness if, obedient to what we have written through the Holy Spirit, you root out the lawless anger of your jealousy, according to the prayer for peace and concord which we have made in this letter. We are sending faithful and discreet men, who have lived amongst us without blame from youth to old age; they will be witnesses between you and us.[4]

[4] Translation from Giles, *op. cit.*

At the beginning of the second century there is other important evidence to be recorded. These are the terms in which St Ignatius of Antioch addresses the Roman Church: "To the Church . . . that presides in the district of the region of the Romans, being worthy of God, worthy of honour, worthy of congratulation, worthy of praise, worthy of success, worthy in purity, and having the presidency of the love, following the law of Christ. . . ."[5]

It was in the year 106 that Ignatius wrote such phrases. Almost thirty-five years later Hermas, the author of the mystical treatise full of strange visions which is known as *The Shepherd*, concluding his work, entrusts to the Bishop of Rome the task of passing it on to all the Churches. A little later Bishop Abercius of Hierapolis, composing his own epitaph before his death, tells therein, in symbolic terms recalling the Apocalypse, that he has gone to Rome at the behest of the holy Shepherd, "to consider and to behold the queen with garment and sandals of gold", and that there he "beheld a people having a shining seal"—baptism.[6] And some years later again, about the year 180, St Irenaeus, Bishop of Lyons, defining the purity of the dogmas against the gnostic heresies, quotes the doctrines of the Church of Rome as a decisive reference: "For to this Church, on account of her more powerful principality, it is necessary (? inevitable) that every Church should come together (? agree), that is the faithful from all sides, in which, always, that which is the tradition from the apostles has been preserved by those who are from all parts."[7] Hegesippus, for his part, declares that he has seen in Rome the centre of an intense Christian life, and carries the list of the succession of its bishops to Anicetus. Dionysius, Bishop of Corinth, in a letter written to the Romans, congratulates their Church on preserving the tomb of the apostles Peter and Paul, and reminds them that the Church of Corinth retains and

[5] Translation from Giles, *op. cit.*
[6] Translation from Giles, *loc. cit.*
[7] Translation from Giles, *loc. cit.*, including the queries; this is a very difficult passage to render, so that Giles quotes the Latin as well.

continues to read the letter addressed to it from Rome by Clement.

The authority of Peter's successors is shown also in the second century in the disputes about the date of Easter. The Asians celebrated the feast of Easter on the fourteenth day of Nisan, or Abib, when the Jews kept the Passover, and Rome celebrated it on the Sunday following the fourteenth day of Nisan. Polycarp, Bishop of Smyrna, deeply attached to the tradition of his Church, made the journey to Rome specially to discuss the question with Anicetus, whose pontificate occurred between 155 and 166. It was agreed that each should remain faithful to the usage of his Church. The two bishops treated each other with the highest esteem. Yet the journey to Rome of so old and venerable a man as Polycarp implies the respect that was felt in Asia for the Bishop of Rome. That respect could be only for the successor of Peter.

The same conclusion can be drawn from the fact that Bishop Dionysius of Corinth, thanking Soter, Bishop of Rome, the successor of Anicetus, about the year 170, for his generous alms to the Churches elsewhere, declared that at Corinth the letter of Pope Clement of which we have already spoken, and which was then already nearly three-quarters of a century old, was still read in the churches on Sundays.

Meanwhile, the dispute about Easter continued. The need for unity was so keenly felt in the Church that real distress was caused by the thought that all the Churches did not celebrate the paschal feast on the same date. The solution of the problem offered by the gentleness of Anicetus did not satisfy everyone. So about 191 Pope Victor wrote to Polycrates, Bishop of Ephesus, to ask him to call together the bishops of Asia and to persuade them to adopt the Roman usage on the question of Easter. Victor assuredly felt a very strong sense of the authority enjoyed by his Church. His language, indeed, was so imperious as to be almost threatening. Polycrates complied with Victor's wishes and assembled the Churches of his part of the world. They were not willing to renounce their usages. Polycrates replied categorically, "I am not affrighted by threats. For those better than I have said, 'We must obey God rather than men.'" But Victor insisted. He sought advice from the other Churches of the East, and, according to Eusebius, synodal letters reached him from the synods of Osrhoene, Gaul, Palestine and Corinth. All these letters declared that the paschal feast must be celebrated on a Sunday. This, it was said, was the usage of Alexandria, which, each year, made the exact date of the solemnity known everywhere. At Alexandria complicated calculations about the Easter moon were made. Victor was right, then, to hold to the Roman practice, which was that of the whole Church, with the exception of the Churches of Ephesus and its neighbourhood. He had threatened Polycrates with excommunication; he carried out his threats, in the end pronouncing the excommunication against all those who did not obey him. But the Bishop of Lyons, Irenaeus, begged the Pope not to carry his severity too far, and his advice prevailed. The Easter controversy was left to take its own course, without leading to a breach between the Churches. The only outcome of it was that Victor had felt himself able to excommunicate Churches that were venerable in their antiquity, and that no one dared to reply that he was exceeding his powers.

What exactly, then, was the opinion of Irenaeus on the subject of the powers of the pope as the successor of St Peter? He gives it in his *Adversus Haereses,* which is usually dated from about the year 180. If Irenaeus had felt the least trace of the hesitation which "biblicism" has conjured up—that is, if he had believed only in the written texts—Irenaeus would have invoked the *Tu es Petrus,* the *Confirma fratres tuos,* the *Pasce oves meas.* For him, however—and in this he is wholly representative of the primitive Church—Catholic truth is handed on from generation to generation *by the medium of tradition.* The teaching that comes from the apostles is the only true teaching. In each Church that teaching is guaranteed by the episcopal succession. Nevertheless, Irenaeus remarks, it would take too long to enumerate the episcopal lists of all the Churches, and, moreover, it would be unnecessary to do so. Why? Because it is enough to recall the episcopal succession *in one Church alone*, the greatest, the most glorious, since it has been founded and established by the blessed apostles Peter and Paul. Of this Church the episcopal list is known. Irenaeus has given it above. And he concludes with an oft-quoted phrase which, unfortunately, we possess only in Latin, although we know that he wrote in Greek: "For to this Church, on account of her more powerful principality, it is necessary (? inevitable) that every Church should come together (? agree), that is the faithful from all sides, in which, always, that which is the tradition from the apostles has been preserved by those who are from all parts."[8]

It is impossible to exaggerate the importance of this text, which comes from a bishop venerable among all others, from a man originally from Asia, a disciple of Polycarp and, through him, of St John; the leader of a Church without close links with Rome, actuated only by a solicitude for the truth and for Christian unity. St Irenaeus specifies that it is necessary to have recourse to the Roman Church and to be in agreement with it. This, according to him, is a moral, religious and, therefore, even a sacred necessity. It is not only a matter of convenience or utility; it is an obligation. The other Churches must be in agreement with the Roman Church, must cooperate with her, and must even when necessary send representatives to her for the settlement of difficulties. "The other Churches"—a phrase which, as Gustave Bardy remarks, means the faithful everywhere.

And why does the Church of Rome possess this signal privilege? Because her "more powerful principality"—*propter potiorem*, or *potentiorem, principilitatem*—comes to her from her foundation by the apostles Peter and Paul. So this "more powerful principality" is not connected with the fact that Rome was also the capital of the Roman Empire, the key-city of a

[8] Migne, *Patrologia Graeca* 7, 848: translation here quoted, with queries, from Giles, *op. cit.*

political civilization, but arises from the fact that that Church was originally founded by Peter, whose name is inseparable from that of Paul. "It is difficult", concludes Mgr Duchesne, "to find a clearer expression (1) of the doctrinal unity of the universal Church; (2) of the sovereign and unique importance of the Roman Church as the witness, guardian and organ of the apostolic tradition; (3) of her superior preeminence among all the Christian communities."[9]

At the beginning of the third century St Callistus, who gave his name to one of the most important of the Roman catacombs, succeeded to the see of Peter. There is no need to enter here in detail into the opposition which he met with on the one hand from St Hippolytus, and on the other hand from Tertullian. It is enough to say that he was reproached for having overthrown the ancient discipline by the relaxations which he introduced. What we must emphasize, however, is that Tertullian describes him ironically as "Bishop of the bishops", and reproaches him in these terms:

> I ask: how do you come to usurp the prerogatives of the Church? If it is because the Lord said to Peter, "Upon this rock I will build my Church, to thee I have given the keys of the heavenly kingdom", or, "Whatsoever thou shalt bind or loose on earth shall be bound or loosed in heaven", do you for that reason presume to have diverted the power of binding and loosing to yourself, that is to every sister Church of Petrine origin? What a fellow you are, subverting and wholly changing the obvious intention of the Lord, who conferred this on Peter personally.[10]

Tertullian rejects, then, the interpretation of the celebrated *Tu es Petrus* text which we accept. But Tertullian, at that date, was a man fallen into heresy; and what remains notable in his language is that, in his very reproach, he recognizes that appeal is beginning to be made, within the Church, to the fundamental texts. St Hippolytus and Tertullian agree in proclaiming that what Callistus does concerns the entire Church. If Callistus has overthrown the ancient discipline, what is notable

[9] Duchesne, *Eglises separées*. 119.
[10] Translation from Giles, *loc. cit.*

is that he has been followed. It is he alone whom Hippolytus and Tertullian regard as responsible, and in so doing they bear witness to the authority which the Bishop of Rome possessed. Callistus, without a shadow of doubt, is the chief among the bishops in their eyes. What is notable, in other words, is that his jurisdiction is not restricted to the confines of his own Church; that to a large extent he has all the other bishops under his control.

A similar field of inquiry concerns the relationship between St Cyprian, Bishop of Carthage in the middle of the third century, and the see of Peter. We need pause only for the essential points. St Cyprian is very much aware of the unity of the Church. In May, 251, he brought out a work which bore the title *De unitate Ecclesiae*, in which he describes the unity that was founded by Christ upon Peter with the words *Tu es Petrus*. And he says clearly, "It is upon one single man that he founds the Church"—*super unum aedificat Ecclesiam*. The phrase should be remembered.

It is certainly true that Cyprian goes on to observe that all the other apostles were endowed with powers similar to those of Peter, in such a manner that in each Church unity rests upon the person of the bishop. Cyprian does not set himself to demonstrate the necessary unity of the Universal Church, but that of each individual Church, under the authority of its bishop. He would contradict himself, however, if he forgot the principle which he stated at the beginning of his argument, "It is upon one single man that he founds the Church." Moreover, in his Letter 48, written to St Cornelius, head of the Church of Rome, St Cyprian says that he recommends all those who go to Rome to recognize in the Church of Rome "the womb and root of the Catholic Church" and to remain loyal to it. In Letter 49 he is still more explicit: speaking of a false bishop who has arisen against him at Carthage, he becomes indignant that this usurper should attempt to win the favour of Cornelius. "They dare", he writes, "to present letters to the see of Peter" (*ad Petri cathedram*) "and to that principal Church whence is borne sacerdotal unity" (*ad Ecclesiam prin-*

cipalem unde unitas sacerdotalis exorta est). These expressions, *Cathedra Petri* and *Ecclesia principalis*, are titles which Cyprian regards as incontestable. In his eyes, then, the Church of Rome is the first of the Churches, *principalis*—which was the word that St Irenaeus had used already. The Church of Rome is "the Chair of Peter". She is the source of sacerdotal unity—that is, of episcopal unity; for the word *sacerdos* meant bishop at this time.

We shall conclude this survey of the earliest evidence of the Roman primacy—and more could be added to it—with a brief account of the affair of the two Dionysiuses.

About the year 255 there existed in Cyrenaica a group of Sabellians, heretics denying any real distinction between the persons of the Holy Trinity. Now the Bishop of Alexandria, Dionysius, exercised a certain authority in this region by virtue of the traditions of his Church. He took energetic action against these heretics. But in speaking of the persons of the Holy Trinity he himself came to express himself in terms which seemed to make the Son a simple creature and to represent him as subordinate and not equal to the Father. That was, in substance, the error which Arius was to spread in the following century. This language surprised some of the best instructed among his faithful. Without asking their bishop for any further explanations, they went to Rome and accused Dionysius of Alexandria before the head of the Church, who was likewise called Dionysius (259–68).

This is evidence of capital importance. Those Egyptians felt no doubt at all. Their Bishop was a considerable personage, the see of Alexandria one of the most ancient in the Church; but they did not hesitate. They knew that there existed a sovereign arbiter in disputes which might arise within the Church, and that that supreme arbiter was the Bishop of Rome.

What happened? Did the Bishop of Rome agree to act as arbiter in this matter? And did the Bishop of Alexandria recognize his authority? The affair followed a smooth course. Dionysius of Rome called a Council without delay. That was already the Roman method of working, and for long centuries it continued to be used. The Council of Rome unanimously condemned the language of Dionysius of Alexandria. The decision was communicated in two letters. In one Dionysius of Rome asks Dionysius of Alexandria for explanations. In the second, addressed to the Church of Alexandria, and without condemning anyone by name, Dionysius of Rome clearly set forth the Christian doctrine of the Trinity. In the following century Athanasius quoted this letter as an unanswerable document. The head of the Church of Rome there speaks, in fact, as a teacher who decides and not as a theologian who discusses. He transmits the apostolic teaching of which he has the sovereign custody. He does already what two hundred years later St Leo the Great did in his letter to Flavian, and, later again, in 681, Pope Agatho in his encyclical against Monothelism.

So all the facts which I have been quoting—and I have quoted only the most important—lead to the same conclusion: the primacy exercised by the Church of Rome.

Generation after generation, it is always the same authority that is exercised, and it is always by the same right that it is exercised. Clement of Rome invokes the authority of Saints Peter and Paul in order to intervene in the contentions of the Church of Corinth. Irenaeus, who is not of Western origin and received his training from a disciple of St John, proclaims the higher authority of the Church of Rome. The violent attacks of St Hippolytus and Tertullian against St Callistus amount implicitly to a recognition of the governing position which this Bishop of Rome occupies in the Church. Cyprian sees in the Church of Rome the source of ecclesiastical unity; Rome is for him, as always in our own eyes, the "Chair of Peter", the principal Church. The story of the two Dionysiuses, of Rome and of Alexandria, ends by proving that the Church of Rome and its head are regarded as the linchpin of Catholic unity. In this last case everything combines to instruct us. The fact that recourse is had to Rome in a theological dispute that arose in Alexandria, that Dionysius of Rome takes action, pronounces sentence, communicates it to the Bishop of Alexandria—and not as he might have given an opinion, not as a matter of local theology, but as Catholic doctrine in its purest form—the fact above all that Dionysius accepts this sentence and feels himself obliged to send to Rome an apology intended to show that he is fully in agreement with the head of that Church, that he admits entirely the doctrine which the head of that Church has enunciated, as being that of the Catholic Church: does not all this demonstrate that evidently from this time the primacy of the Church of Rome is recognized outside Rome, and represents the mainspring in the life of the Church?

To sum up. The preeminence of the successors of Peter has two foundations in Christian history: tradition and Scripture. In juridical language—which, however, is not literally applicable in this connection—one might speak of the customary law and the written law. In the very first days of the Church, after the visible departure of our Lord from this earth, tradition —that is, customary law—was the only source of the pontifical authority. This is the period in which we have spoken of the *élan vital* in the Church. The Church was not founded by a written charter, on texts authorized and known to all. She was founded upon a sort of living chain: God, Christ, the apostles, the bishops. By the will of Jesus one of his twelve disciples was three times invested with a special charge. He even received this mission by the symbol of the name which Jesus conferred on that apostle at the time of his first appearance before him. This disciple was Simon, become Peter-Kephas, the Rock, the Man-Rock, the foundation-stone.

Peter exercised this authority after the departure of our Lord from this earth. He retained it throughout his travels and then throughout his life in Rome. He was to transmit it to those who would succeed him at the head of the Church of Rome, become the "president of the Christian brotherhood". Such was the verbal charter of the Christian Church, its living tradition, its customary law.

When the Gospels had been written, and recognized by the

Church as inspired by God, this verbal charter was reinforced with a written charge. As the Church advanced in age and left her first beginnings far behind, the written proofs of the authority of the Church of Rome, such as it had been since the death of Peter, were multiplied. These proofs constitute, then, the written charter of the Church, her written law. Henceforward custom and biblical authority, customary law and written law, come together, fuse into one, are but one. Agreement is complete.

No arguments arose against the Roman primacy, or, when they did, were only fleeting clouds, soon dispersed. A Polycrates of Ephesus, a Hippolytus of Rome, a Tertullian could raise objections or formulate contrary opinions. Unity in the Church was maintained despite them and against them. It was only very much later, and under the pressure of considerations which we shall shortly consider, that two great schisms were produced and that Christ's seamless robe was rent. Such was the Catholic, Apostolic and Roman Church at the time of St Peter. Such is she still at the end of twenty centuries.

CHAPTER IV

THE TASKS OF THE PAPACY

As I said in the introduction to this little book, there can be no
question here of sketching, even in its broadest outline, the
whole history of the papacy from its beginning to our own
time. I have dwelt at some length on its origins and its opening
years because I have thought it useful to give special attention,
in however elementary a fashion, to the reasoning, facts and
proofs on which we base our belief in the authority of the See
of Peter. The Catholic hierarchy is so necessary to the Church,
it represents in our eyes such a condition of her safe keeping,
that the importance of establishing the legitimacy of that hierarchy cannot be exaggerated. But to follow the development
of the papacy step by step from the first heads of the Church
of Rome to our own days would be too great a task to attempt
in these few pages. The history of the papacy and the history
of the Church are bound up together. Other volumes in this
present series are devoted to this majestic theme. They treat
in particular of the theological disputes which have followed
one another through the centuries. I will not enter in any detail,
therefore, into the succession of pontificates which, between
St Peter and John XXIII, forms a chain with 259 links. I propose to do no more than recall the essential tasks to which the
endeavours of the popes were directed in the first centuries of
Christianity; to indicate, in terms of the history of the papacy,
the principal turning-points of the Christian era; and finally to
try to describe the position of the papacy in the world of today.
Through many storms, vicissitudes and ordeals, this astound-
ing continuity is summed up in the one formula, the papacy,

the guardian of the deposit of faith. There is nothing else at all like it in the history of mankind. How can we fail to see it as a supernatural sign?

It may be said that during the first centuries of the Christian era four essential duties confronted the papacy:

1. To overcome ceaselessly recurring heresies.
2. To resist the barbarian invasions.
3. To organize and extend the missionary work of the Church.
4. To defend the authority of the see of Peter against encroachments of the Empire.

These four principal tasks are not sharply distinguishable from one another; quite the reverse, they are inextricably interrelated and entangled. The popes have had to defend the deposit of which they have the custody simultaneously against deviations and usurpations—Ariel and Caliban; and this was the danger, which without the promises of Christ would have been mortal, that threatened to stifle the Church in her cradle. The extraordinary multiplication of heresies is the most striking phenomenon of the first Christian period. "Heresy", wrote Mgr Duchesne, "is contemporary with the Gospel. Hardly is the Father's field sown before cockle shows itself there alongside the good grain." In the first Churches there were already Judaizing gnostics who heralded the incursion of philosophical gnosticism.

It was at Samaria, the rival of Jerusalem, that Gnosticism made its appearance in Christian history. Simon Magus was the first of the heresiarchs. A whole series of leaders of sects followed him, each elaborating his own system and teaching his own theology. Successively there were—I mention only the chief ones—Meander of Capparteus, Dositheus, Cleobius, Saturninus of Antioch; then, in Egypt, Valentinus, Basilides,

Carpocrates (whose reputation was great), Cerdo, Marcion and Florimus.

St Irenaeus and Hippolytus have described these principal heresies. Hardly had one had its day than it was succeeded by another. It is a miracle that the delicate young tree which was the Church was not overwhelmed by this advancing jungle; that her development, the extension of her influence, were not interrupted. Such circumstances were to recur again and again throughout history. The day came, alas, when Christian unity was broken; but the Church was nevertheless strong enough by then to bear those grievous wounds. Schisms certainly wound her; they check her, limit her progress in the world; but they cannot endanger her.

October 28th, 312, is a key date not only for Christianity but for the history of the world. In Rome on that day, near the Milvian bridge which bestrides the Tiber, a battle upon which the fate of the Empire was to depend took place between those who disputed mastery of it. Constantine, the son of Constantius Chlorus, at the head of forty thousand Gauls, Germans and Britons, routed the army of a hundred thousand Italians and African mercenaries commanded by Maxentius, the son of Maximian, who had had himself proclaimed as Emperor, Augustus, deposing Maximian II. Maxentius died, drowned in the Tiber, and Constantine triumphed in Rome. On the eve of the battle he had invoked the protection of Christ, to whom he attributed his victory. When he had gained all power as a ruler, while not living as a Christian—he was baptized only when at the point of death—but combining Christian sympathies with an oriental paganism, Constantine opened a new era in the history of Christianity.

Not only were the persecutions to which Christians had been subjected brought to an end—Diocletian had abdicated only a few years beforehand—but the Edict of Milan, in February or March, 313, solemnly accorded to Christians the freedom which the Empire had always refused them: "We desire that whoever desires to follow the Christian religion shall be able to do so without any fear of disturbance. Christians have full freedom to follow their religion."

In 323, when he had overcome Licinius, Constantine became the sole Emperor, the absolute master, and carried his support of the Christians still further. He openly favoured the Christian religion, entrusted high responsibilities to Christians, built Christian basilicas, and, in particular, built the basilica of St Peter in Rome, in the remarkable circumstances of which we have already spoken. He took part, moreover, in the struggles in which the Church was to engage against the heresies. Indeed, he concerned himself so closely with these struggles—and his immediate successors were to follow this example so strongly—that a new danger soon faced the Church, that of the encroachment of the imperial power in a field that did not concern it.

Events, then, imposed a twofold vigilance on the successors of St Peter: a twofold mission which was to play a major part in the unfolding of Christian history.

The continual assault of the heresies against the doctrine left by Christ and spread by the young Church, and the continual victory of that Church against the heresies, represented, as I have just said, a kind of miracle. That miracle, desired by God, was the essential work of the papacy, the deepest reason for its existence.[1] Thus no sooner had the Church obtained the grace that she needed in order to expand than she was at grips with the twofold danger of the encroachment of the imperial power and the assaults of heresy. Looking back over the history of the first seven hundred years of the Church's history we see her contending with the major heresies threatening the very foundations of the Christian faith; no sooner had she dealt with Arianism and Subordinationism than she must turn her attention to Pelagianism, and then Nestorianism followed closely by Monophysitism and Monothelitism. Great names flit across the pages of her history—Athanasius is sent into exile and returns only to be exiled again; Augustine demolishes the Pelagians; Sophronius, a monk of Palestine, speaks out against Monothelitism. But in all this troubled history one fact emerges

[1] A full account of the struggle against the heresies together with an analysis of their tenets will be found in Volume 136 of this series.

with astonishing clarity—constantly recourse is had to the see of Peter for judgement, for the definition of what is the orthodox faith, and if a General Council issues decrees settling a dispute, drawing up a creed, they are subject to the approval of Peter's successor and so bear the stamp of the apostolic see. Sylvester, Innocent I and Leo the Great—to mention but three —dominate the scene.

So the Church, during the first centuries of her life, never ceased, if we may so put it, to be a target for heresy. Despite incidents and accidents, doctrine always remained safe. The authority of the head of the Roman Church was recognized and invoked in every part of the Christian world. Appeal was constantly made to it. Those who flouted its decisions exposed themselves to excommunication. To challenge it was at the same time to acknowledge it. And even if that authority knew moments of weakness—under a Liberius or a Honorius—these arose only from individual human circumstances, quickly repaired. What was to be known as the papacy—that is, the whole notion of the continuity of the pontifical power—stands out in increasing clarity as the Church grows.

Although defence of the Faith is the most important of the tasks committed to the successor of St Peter, and although this defence was unremittingly sustained through the early centuries of Christianity, it was not the only task for which the successive heads of the Church were responsible. They had another, just as compelling, which was to preserve the life of the new-born Church, not only her doctrinal and spiritual life, but her very existence.

When at length the early Christians gained their freedom and a creative era dawned for the Church, an uninterrupted succession of tragic events—the unspeakable disorders which broke out in the West caused by the barbarian invasions, the decadence of the Empire, the ambitions of the kings of the Visigoths and of the Ostrogoths, the onslaught of the Vandals —exposed that Church, and the see of Peter, to the gravest of

dangers. It is miraculous that she was able to withstand the
proliferation of heresies which threatened to stifle her from
the time of Christ's ascension onwards; it is almost more wonderful to see how she overcame all the various onslaughts
which assailed her during this long period of political disintegration, the migrations of populations, anarchy, uncertainty
and violence. Above all, it is wonderful to observe the extraordinary rôle played by this frail institution in the midst of
violence and destructive instincts. It was a fundamental and a
saving rôle.

The unity of the Church depended ultimately upon the
Roman primacy. The part played by the papacy in saving the
unity of civilization is therefore fundamental. It is in this sense
that we must admire the greatness of such outstanding men
as St Leo the Great and St Gregory the Great.

Leo the Great not only faced the danger of heresy in the
East, he also confronted Attila in Italy and then, following
the horrors of the Vandal invasion, restored Rome. It was the
popes who came forward as the defenders of the West against
Theodoric, King of the Ostrogoths, just as against the Byzantine rulers of Italy in the sixth century and the bitter onslaughts of the Lombards. Among them was Gregory the
Great, who ruled the Church from 590 to 604, and whose
reign may serve as a model to illustrate the work of St Peter's
successors.

Gregory the Great realized that the hope of the world rested
in the Roman primacy. He did everything in his power to assert
and to exercise that primacy. In Italy he upheld his right to
confirm the election of the Bishop of Ravenna, in defiance of
the Byzantine Governor of that city. He affirmed his jurisdiction over Sevinus, Patriarch of Aquileia, and Natalis, Metropolitan of Salona. In the East he protested against the title of
"Ecumenical Patriarch" assumed by the Patriarch of Constantinople, John the Faster. The break between Rome and
Byzantium was complete for a time, but Gregory's strong words
were not without avail. A short time after his death, in 607, a
more orthodox Emperor deprived the Syrian Patriarch, the

successor of John the Faster, of the title of "Ecumenical" and recognized the primacy of the Holy See. At the same time Gregory the Great negotiated with the Lombards in Italy, with the Franks in Gaul and with the Visigoths in Spain. He made the authority of Peter's successor recognized everywhere. He sent the first great mission to England and paved the way for Christian unity among the warrior princes who divided that country between them. Finally, during the disorder which threatened to overrun the whole Italian peninsula, he practically took the place of the Exarch of Ravenna; he extended and strengthened the Church's patrimony; he became the father of the peoples throughout the already extensive territories of the papacy. He laid the foundations of the future "temporal power" of the popes.

For it was gradually and as though by force of circumstances that the popes became the heads of a small temporal state. Enriched at the beginning by the gifts of the faithful, the Church of Rome possessed a territorial patrimony at a very early date. In the time of Gregory the Great this patrimony covered some five thousand square kilometres, or nearly two thousand square miles. This was the kernel of what was later called the Duchy of Rome. The reigning pope was but its administrator, and handed on that position to his successors.

The papacy had to defend these possessions, which belonged also to the poor, against the ambitions of those within and without. In the seventh century the Lombards threatened its integrity. The popes protested and negotiated, but without result. They appealed to the Byzantine Emperor but no help was forthcoming from that quarter. Nevertheless the Church's independence had to be safeguarded, and to that end a Christian protector had to be found and won over to the cause. Who was it to be? The Lombards had indeed been converted to Catholicism; but, although they recognized the spiritual authority of the pope, they had less respect for the Church's possessions. Moreover, the Romans felt an almost physical aversion for them. According to reliable historians, this was not without its influence on the policy of the popes.

It was in 753 that Stephen II (752–7) decided to ask the Franks for help, following an exchange of letters with their ruler, Pepin the Short, and the Emperor of Byzantium. In good faith Stephen II went first of all to the court of Astulf, King of the Lombards, to obtain from him the necessary guarantees for Rome. This approach failed. The Lombards could not conceal their ambitions. They dreamed of seizing Rome and making it their capital. Continuing his journey, Stephen II crossed the Alps and went to Ponthion, near Vitry-le-François, where Pepin the Short was living. He arrived on January 6th, 754, and was received with the utmost respect and veneration by the King of the Franks. The pope knelt before him and asked for his aid "in settling the troubles of Peter and of the republic of the Romans". The King at once raised the pope to his feet and promised his assistance in the task of "obliging the Exarchate of Ravenna to restore the rights and the lands of the republic".

Pepin the Short at once sent an emissary to Astulf, but obtained no result. He sent a second, and then a third—both equally unsuccessful. He then decided to send a military expedition. Before this the pope—still at Ponthion—had consecrated Pepin and his two sons, on July 28th, 754, the first instance of the consecration of a king on the soil of France, renewing and confirming the consecration conferred, with the pope's permission, by St Boniface in 752.

In 755 Astulf, having been defeated, sued for peace, which was granted him on the following three conditions:

1. The pope should have the free enjoyment of his territories in Lombardy;
2. Free possession of the Duchy of Rome;
3. The surrender to the pope—and not to Byzantium—of the Exarchate of Ravenna, which had been usurped by the Lombards.

In the following year, however, a second expedition by the

Franks was necessary to compel Astulf to observe the terms of the peace.[2]

Such were the beginnings of the Papal States. The alliance of the papacy and the Franks was, as we see, at the root of them. Without entering into the details of the history of those States we may recall that their constitution was confirmed and extended by Charlemagne in 774 and 787. The consequences of this important event were broadly these:

1. The popes considered themselves released from their dependence on Byzantium;

2. They tried to establish durable frontiers for their States by including within them the possessions that remained inside Lombard territory;

3. They constantly had to guard, on the one hand, against possible abuses of the Frankish protectorate and, on the other, against the ambitions of the Roman princes who wanted to capture the pontifical power for the sake of the resources of the States administered by that power. For a short period it was the Counts of Tusculum who made and unmade the popes. Disturbances were a regular feature in Rome. The Roman pontiff had to appeal to the German emperors to restore order and to safeguard his authority. This help, however, was not given disinterestedly. The struggles between the papacy and the empire—and the empires—went on for centuries under various guises and with varying fortunes. That was the papacy's third ordeal.

After the heresies, after the persecutions, after the barbarian invasions, the papacy had to defend its independence. As that independence increased new difficulties threatened it. That was

[2] The tradition which gives France the title of the "Eldest daughter of the Church" also has its origin in this event. In fact, in recognition of the great service rendered to the papacy by Pepin the Short, Stephen II adopted his two sons and gave them symbolically as "sister" the relics of St Petronilla, the daughter (whether carnal or spiritual) of St Peter. These relics, which were kept in Rome, were regarded as the most precious in the Church's possession. France accordingly became "the sister of Petronilla", and consequently the eldest daughter of St Peter, the founder of the Church. So came the title of "Eldest daughter of the Church".

the price of its astonishing success. What strikes one even on
glancing at these events is how regularly and in what timely
fashion the papacy detached itself from these convulsive move-
ments of the world. For the world was in a state of ceaseless
movement. Christian civilization gradually replaced that of
Rome.

> The eighth century [writes Daniel-Rops] was one of the turn-
> ing points of history and, although the events of that century
> were not of a nature to cause sudden changes such as those of
> the previous centuries, it was by far the most important century
> of all the period with which we are concerned. Did not the con-
> ceptions which it evolved influence all the Middle Ages, secure
> the successes and pose the most serious of all problems? And it
> is apparent that the Church was involved in this new attitude of
> mind from the very outset. The first of these new conceptions
> was that a fresh basis must be found for the political system of
> the West. The Roman conception of the state, founded on the
> experience of a thousand years of law and practice, had col-
> lapsed; the right of force, the *Faustrecht* of the invasions, no
> longer sufficed as a foundation of order. Where could new foun-
> dations be found? A new movement of thought was to give the
> answer, was to absorb the notion of the state within the Church
> and the Christian idea.

The consecration of Charlemagne on Christmas Day in the
year 800, in St Peter's Basilica at Rome, is a date as important
in history as the battle of the Milvian Bridge in 312: or, more
exactly, these dates complement one another. The second is
the fulfilment of the first. With Charlemagne dominating the
West, the West becomes essentially Christian. Christian civilization is established. But, in the words of M. Arquillère, "it
was not long before a prodigious transfer of authority took
place. At the beginning of the ninth century the control of
the Christian West was in the hands of the emperor, and less
than fifty years after the death of Charlemagne it passed into
the hands of Pope Nicholas I (858–67)." "This development",
observes Daniel-Rops, "was the result of the very conditions
under which Charlemagne had conceived and created his empire." What bond did he intend to establish between all the

peoples who had submitted to his armies? Baptism. Was it not logical that the Church, the dispenser of baptismal grace, should come to exercise supreme authority over these peoples?

As Christian civilization progressed and penetrated the complex of public and social life, as the Church became conscious of her enormous authority, as states and social groups improved their new ways of life, clashes were bound to come. The task of the papacy was fraught only with greater responsibilities and greater difficulties. Soon Christian unity was to suffer its first great blow—the schism of the East. Five centuries later it suffered the second—the Protestant Revolution. We shall recall these two great crises in turn, but first we must give a brief historical account of the struggles which brought the priesthood and the empire into conflict, the Church and her secular arm. Whatever may have been the high points and the low, the errors, the excesses of this period of uncertainty, the inherent weaknesses of humanity, one thing is certain: the papacy never lost its preeminence.

It was Leo IX who took up the struggle for the complete independence of the papacy against the empire. Proposed for the papacy by the Emperor Henry III at the Diet of Worms, Leo IX declared wisely that he would only regard himself as the supreme Head of the Church when the clergy and people of Rome had confirmed the choice by giving it their approval. This twofold sanction having been accorded to him, the new pope lost no time in publishing, through Councils in Rome, Rheims and Mainz, decrees against simony and concubinage among the clergy. His successors, Victor II (1055–57), Stephen IX (1057–8) followed the same road. Nicholas II (1059–61) did still better. At the Council of Rome on April 13th, 1059, he published a decree reserving the right of appointing the pope to the cardinal-bishops alone, subject to the agreement of the rest of the clergy and the approval of the emperor. The inspiration behind these measures came from Hildebrand, a most energetic monk, who became pope himself in 1073 under the name of Gregory VII, and is one of the greatest figures in the history of the Church.

Gregory VII's first act was to assert the independence of the pontifical see towards the emperor. He sent Henry IV only a brief announcement of his election. It was his undoubted wish that there should be peaceful cooperation between the Church and the empire. But he intended to remain the sole master of decisions which he regarded as the rightful province of the Church. If it should be necessary, he was determined not to shrink from a clash with the emperor on the question of granting ecclesiastical titles. Gregory was determined at all costs that simony—that is, the sale of bishoprics to the highest bidder, a practice shamelessly followed by the emperor— should disappear. Simony brought in its train what was called "Nicolaism", or concubinage among the clergy.

During this struggle of a hundred different aspects, it fell to Gregory VII to depose the emperor, in 1076, absolving his subjects from the oath of allegiance to him. And such was the pope's prestige that he obliged the emperor to humiliate himself before him, at Canossa in January 1077.

More than one volume would be required to describe the vicissitudes of this first phase of the conflict between the Church and the empire. I confine myself to drawing attention to its extreme importance. This vast conflict came to an end in 1122 with the Concordat of Worms. The Emperor Henry V, son and successor of Henry IV, there declared: "I restore to the Roman Church all possessions and rights which, from the beginning of this conflict to this day, either in my father's reign or in mine, have been taken from St Peter, providing that these possessions are under my control at the present time."

It was in the twelfth and thirteenth centuries that papal power in the West reached its highest point. It was then that what was called the theory of the two swords took root in Western Christendom.

In order to understand it, it is necessary to enter into the spirit of the period. A very great saint of the twelfth century, Bernard of Clairvaux, expressed it thus: "The two swords belong to St Peter. One, the spiritual sword, is in his hand; the other, the temporal sword, is at his command whenever it is necessary to draw it. Peter in fact was told, regarding the sword which seemed the least appropriate to him, 'Put thy sword back into its sheath' (John 18.11). It was not for him, therefore, to use it with his own hands."[3]

Innocent III quite legitimately took the title of "Vicar of Jesus Christ and Successor of the Prince of the Apostles". But from this traditional formula he deduced a theocratic doctrine; he was "the vicar of him whose kingdom has no boundaries". He was "the representative of him to whom belong the earth and all that it contains and all those who inhabit it". He proclaimed that "on ascending the throne of Peter he received the power to overthrow, destroy, disperse, dispel, build and found".

This does not mean that the pope claimed to be able to destroy princes. But he declared himself to be their judge: "Not only have we been placed among the princes," said he, "but, since it belongs to us to judge them, we have been placed above them." His conception of the papal power was that of a "super-power", in the sense that the princes had authority in temporal matters only, whereas the pope had authority over both the temporal and the spiritual. "To the princes", he wrote, "has been given power on earth; to the Church has been given power both on earth and in heaven. The power of the former concerns the body only; that of the latter concerns both body and soul."

One finds similar statements among the successors of Innocent II, notably Gregory IX (1227–41) and, above all, Innocent IV (1243–54).

It need hardly be said that this theocratic doctrine could not fail to provoke strong objections on the part of the princes. In practice, while the popes proclaimed themselves to be "judges of the princes" as of other Christians, they did not seek to interfere in purely political matters. Nevertheless, friction and even conflicts constantly occurred. In the time of Boniface VIII the theocratic doctrine was openly attacked. In 1297

[3] Migne, *P.L.* 216, 1066.

King Philip the Fair indicated to the legates of the pope "that in matters of temporal government he recognized no higher authority than his own".

The pope in no way modified his claims on this account, and in October 1301 he wrote to the King of Hungary: "In his position as supreme Head of the hierarchy the Roman Pontiff has been placed above kings and kingdoms in the Church militant; he therefore has authority over all mortals. Seated on the throne of judgement, he pronounces his sentences with calm and banishes all evil from his sight."

The terms of the Bull *Ausculta, fili,* addressed to the King of France on December 5th, 1301, concerning the affair of the Bishop of Pamiers, Bernard Saisset, are therefore not surprising: "Those who tell you that you have no superior and that you are not subject to the supreme Hierarch of the Church are deceiving you and are outside the fold of the Good Shepherd." And Boniface VIII continued to claim the right and the duty to watch over the eternal salvation of princes no less than that of other Christians.

This spiritual concern led him to intervene in temporal matters in so far as they occasioned sin; for the boundary between the two domains is tenuous. It was particularly so in that period. The pope thought the King of France was violating Christian morality by his seizure of ecclesiastical property, by his fiscal measures and by his oppression of the Church in Lyons. Boniface VIII deemed that he had a right to threaten him with sanctions.

In November, 1302, the pope accordingly convened a Council in Rome. It was in this assembly that he drew up the famous Bull *Unam sanctam,* which, although it contained nothing new, summarized and expounded the doctrine of the two swords, which had been generally accepted in the Church since the time of St Bernard.

Nevertheless, wishing to formulate a dogmatic definition based on the discussions, Boniface VIII at the end of the Bull no longer spoke of the two swords; instead, he produced a formula which was later found to agree with milder theories of the sovereign authority of the popes: "We declare, state, define and pronounce that it is altogether necessary to salvation for every human creature to be subject to the Roman Pontiff."

The reply of the King of France is well known. Philip the Fair let loose a flood of violent accusations against Boniface VIII, and announced his intention of forcing the pope to appear before a General Council, there to be sentenced to deposition.

These were the events which led up to what is known in history as "the Anagni outrage", when the pope was attacked in his palace at Anagni by Philip's chancellor and was taken prisoner. But Boniface VIII was inflexible. To the end he proclaimed: "The saint of Israel is the vicar of God, is the successor of him to whom it was said: 'Thou art Peter and upon this rock I will build my Church.'" A month after the events at Anagni Boniface VIII died, in October 1303.

Although the totalitarian doctrine of the dual power of the popes was defended in that period by such famous theologians as Giles of Rome and Agostino Trionfo, it had nevertheless sustained a great blow.

So for five centuries, from the coronation of Charlemagne to the pontificate of Boniface VIII, Christian civilization had been developed to the advantage, I venture to say, of a maximal interpretation of the authority of the Holy See. Save in the East, the papacy overcame one by one all obstacles confronting it. It became the leading power in the West. But during these five centuries, when the Church had a monopoly in the civilization which was being built, the states, or more precisely, some states, themselves emerged from the uncertainties and changing conditions of the Middle Ages. They were becoming organized. New relationships between the civil powers and the priesthood were coming into existence. A new system was about to be worked out, not without difficulties nor without a dramatic turn of events.

It is thus that there is to be found here and there a progressive secularization of institutions. This spirit is manifested in Germany, where, after the violent conflict between Louis of Bavaria and the popes, Charles IV broke with the past in the famous Golden Bull of January 13th, 1356, which governed the election of the emperors and suppressed by simple omission any papal intervention therein. In France the royal jurisdiction continued to be extended at the expense of ecclesiastical rights from the time of what is known as the Assembly of Vincennes (1329). Little regard was paid to the privileges of the clergy. The king's officers judged and sentenced clergy in spite of the protests of the popes. In England the Statute of Provisors (February 9th, 1351) and the Statute of Praemunire (September 25th, 1353) limited the papal prerogatives and forbade appeal to the tribunals of the Roman Curia. Finally, on the pretext that the popes had become "the chaplains of the King of France", the Lords and Commons absolved King Edward III from the payment of the dues sent by the Crown to the Roman Pontiff since the time of John Lackland. In Italy the lords and the towns took advantage of the pope's absence to become independent.

For the pope had left Rome, and his departure was to be the cause of a very grave crisis, enduring for a century or more. Clement V (1305–14) was a weak man. In order to avoid legal action against Boniface VIII, he had yielded to the King of France in the affair of the Templars and suppressed that order at the Ecumenical Council of Vienne (1309). Alarmed at the constant disorders in his capital, he decided to leave for France. He made his way to Avignon, where he intended his stay to be only temporary. In fact the papacy remained at Avignon for sixty-eight years. Some good popes succeeded him there, including Benedict XII, who was responsible for building the Palace of the Popes, and Clement VI, who purchased the town and territory of Avignon from Joanna of Naples.

To the credit of the Avignon popes must go their consistent efforts to organize the Roman administration, to centralize its affairs and to reform abuses. That period saw the foundation of the Apostolic Camera, for financial matters; the Chancery, for relations with princes; the organization of justice in the Consistory or at the tribunal of the Rota; and the Penitentiary. But the extended absence of the popes from the city of Rome, of which they remained the bishops, nevertheless had regrettable consequences. Serious disturbances took place during the election of Urban VI in 1378, and were followed by a real schism.

Elected under the pressure of the disturbances in Rome, Urban VI was neither patient nor skilful. Most of the cardinals to whom he owed his election deserted him. They asserted that, as the choice had not been free, the election was void, and they proceeded to elect a new pope—an anti-pope—who took the name of Clement VI and returned to Avignon. Thenceforward there were two popes: the pope of Rome, who retained many supporters, and the pope of Avignon, acknowledged by France, Scotland, Castile, Savoy, Portugal, Aragon and Naples.

The whole Church was in anguish. Where was the true pope? An almost unbelievable quantity of pamphlets, treatises, lampoons, reports, university debates and so on, began to appear in support of both sides, not to mention false prophecies, visions and alleged revelations. In 1394, sixteen years after the beginning of the schism, the University of Paris, the most illustrious in Christendom, arranged a sort of referendum on the way to bring this calamitous state of affairs to an end. More than ten thousand replies were received, proposing these among other means:

1. A recourse to arms, the *via facti*;
2. A recourse to diplomacy, the *via reductionis intrusi*;
3. A juridical discussion between the two popes, the *via conventionis vel discussionis*;
4. The voluntary abdication of both popes, the *via cessionis*;
5. Arbitration, the *via compromissi*; and finally
6. Recourse to a General Council, the *via Concilii*.

After long argument the last solution carried the day, leading to an unexpected result. The Council which met at Pisa in

1409 declared both the rival popes deposed as schismatics, and nominated another one. As the two popes concerned would not accept this decision, each retaining his own resolute supporters, there were henceforward three popes instead of two. Far from remedying the situation, what had been done had made it worse.

A new Council met at Constance in 1414, having been called by the pope of Pisa (John XXIII), and at its fourth and fifth sessions it proclaimed the superiority of the Council over the pope, a thesis which became the basis of what was afterwards known as theological Gallicanism.

In the end, owing to the voluntary abdication of the pope of Rome, and after many discussions and events, the Council was able to elect a new pope. This was Martin V (1417–31). This time the entire Church recognized him, in spite of the obstinacy of the pope of Avignon, who, though without supporters, to the end refused to abdicate.

The Council of Constance closed on April 22nd, 1418. It had accomplished a very necessary task, but it burdened the papacy with a heavy mortgage: the doctrine of the superiority of the Council over the pope. It was the negation of the centuries-old tradition of the Church. The popes who followed were anxious to revert to the traditional teaching. In approving the decrees of the Council of Constance, Martin V devised a prudent formula enabling him to except the findings of the fourth and fifth sessions; but he was unable to prevent the convocation of the Council of Basle, in 1431. His successor, Eugenius IV (1431–47), who had begun by confirming the meeting of the Council, soon came into conflict with it. He wanted to dissolve it. The Council resisted. It went so far as to proclaim him deposed, and nominated an anti-pope. Eugenius IV was unshaken by this opposition. He convened another Council at Florence, which achieved reunion with the Greeks although unhappily it lasted only a few years. The dissidence caused by the Council of Basle came to an end in 1449 with the complete submission of the anti-pope—the last in history. The papacy and the Church had thus passed through an extremely critical period. Yet grave dangers still remained. The doctrine of the superiority of the Council had not been suppressed, and Luther's revolt was soon to be supported, in the first instance, by the principle of this superiority. Other and even graver dangers lay ahead.

After six centuries of development Christian civilization was passing through a period of crisis. All kinds of ideas and customs were in a state of flux. There were, of course, beneficial elements in this evolutionary process. Thus, the popes sought agreement with kings and princes no longer by imposing their authority, as in the Middle Ages, in the name of the principle of the two swords, but by direct negotiations, by means of Concordats. They even went to the length of suppressing elections to the major benefices (bishoprics and abbeys) in order to leave them at the disposal of sovereigns, reserving to themselves only the right of canonical installation. Certainly they also pursued grandiose political aims in trying to prolong the idea of the crusade in which the papacy had taken the initiative in the time of Urban II. They remained its last champions because of the threat offered by the Turks to the Christian powers at variance.

It must be frankly admitted, moreover, that alongside the marvellous artistic flowering of the Renaissance, the papacy was to pass through the darkest period in its history. The morals of the period did not spare the Roman Curia. Perhaps it was necessary for it to sink to such depths, in order to react and to recover its purity and its soul. St Peter himself denied Christ three times in the courtyard of the High Priest.

The Church was to pay for these serious shortcomings by a particularly severe and painful ordeal in the shape of the Protestant Revolution. Before glancing at that, however, we must go back five centuries and first consider the schism which had separated from Rome most of the Christians in the East.

CHAPTER V

FROM THE EASTERN SCHISM TO TRENT

The story of the papacy is perhaps comparable to a symphony which its composer bases on several themes. There is the theme of the heresies, the theme of the persecutions, the theme of the invasions, the theme of the usurpations, the theme of the struggles for independence, the theme of the reorientations. All these alternate, blend and follow upon one another, merge into one another, disappear and reappear, sometimes fortissimo, sometimes muted. At no time are they absent. In seeking to reconstruct their history we must discriminate among the mass of facts, retaining only those which are the most significant and decisive. But if in a comprehensive study this necessity inevitably means a distortion of the reality, to what mutilations must it not lead in a book like this with no other ambition than to be a rapid guide to the centuries?

We go back five centuries, then, to consider the unhappy schism which so completely separated the Eastern Church from Rome that no signs of reconciliation appear even to this day. The two names of Photius and Michael Cerularius are an apt summary of the whole affair.

Strictly speaking, the origins of this separation go much further back than the second half of the ninth century. They were of a highly complex nature, were more political than doctrinal and are bound up with the transformation which took place after the end of the domination of Rome, when the

Empire became Christian, and "ecumenical", though the Church that had taken root in Rome yet remained Roman.

Fr Congar, in a remarkable study of the Eastern Schism which he published under the title of *Neuf cents ans après*, wrote:

> The schism seems to us to have been brought about by the acceptance of a situation in which each part of the Christian world lived, acted and judged without taking the other into account. Remoteness, provincialism, a condition of "no relations", a state of reciprocal ignorance (this is an expression of Fr M. Jugie's), all of which can be expressed by the estrangement. The Eastern Schism came about as the result of a progressive "estrangement", and was made formal by the acceptance of that estrangement. [. . .]
>
> Thus the relations between Rome and Constantinople often presented the occasion for rivalry and competition of a kind which sometimes had juridical and political aspects (Illyricum, Bulgaria), but was fundamentally ecclesiological in character. The Roman conception was of a universal Church, centred around her primacy. In this she responded to her profound vocation, founded on the institution by our Lord and on the apostolic presence of Peter and Paul. She was likewise favoured by various politico-natural forces—Roman genius, the ideological and sentimental heritage of Imperial Rome, the fact that in a West occupied by the Barbarians, Rome appeared as a centre of civilization, and even as its only source. Among peoples who did not set up against her the barriers of a secular culture and a Christian Church already in existence, she had a clear field for establishing the life of a Church that would be one, would be Latin, and, on a last analysis, Roman. By contrast, Christianity in the East had developed from the beginning amid varying regional cultures with very ancient roots. To the extent that Constantinople was predominant (and this varied with the changes of political fortune) it was the idea of an imperial Church, ecumenical in that sense, which prevailed. At the same time, the existence of autonomous local Churches with their own liturgical languages had from the beginning tended towards the idea of a communion or brotherhood of Churches. Historical vicissitudes, the aggressive impact of Islam, led Byzantium to become uncompromising, like a nation confronted by other

national powers, and the Byzantine Church to become a Greek national Church. The idea of a Church organized on a universal basis, with a hierarchy conceived correspondingly, had scarcely a chance of taking root in Eastern minds.

These considerations indicate the deeper meaning of the separation which was to come.

The Byzantine Emperors still retained a theoretical sovereignty over the West, despite their powerlessness to exercise it and their inability to defend the papacy against the Lombard invasions. The long iconoclastic quarrels, first from 735 to 787, and then from 815 to 843, had ranged the popes, the guardians of orthodoxy, against several of these Byzantine Caesars. When Leo III reestablished the Western Empire it was regarded in Constantinople as a veritable treason. Charlemagne's imperial title was only recognized by Byzantium belatedly and with repugnance. In addition there was continual friction between Rome and Constantinople over the boundaries assigned to the two patriarchates in the Balkan Peninsula. Finally, and perhaps principally, it had become usual at Byzantium to regard all western Europeans as "barbarians" and to despise everything connected with ancient Rome. So it was that the idea of catholicity gradually disappeared in the East.

The patriarchs at Constantinople, no less than the popes, had been obliged to struggle against the abuses of imperial protection. But they had not always succeeded in maintaining their independence from the state. All these considerations must be borne in mind if the lamentable rupture consummated in 1054 is to be understood.

Schism had already occurred under Photius, a man of vast erudition and powerful intelligence who, by order of the Emperor, had illegally taken the place of the Patriarch Ignatius. In 863 Nicholas I had declared his election void and welcomed the converted Bulgarians into the Roman Church, addressing to them a celebrated document which contained 106 replies to their questions. Photius accepted neither of these papal decisions. He caused the pope to be declared a heretic by the Synod of Constantinople in 867. But in the same year Photius himself was deposed by a new Emperor, who renewed relations with Rome. This schism had lasted four years. In 869 the eighth Ecumenical Council reestablished Catholic unity, while reserving the rights of Byzantium over the Bulgars. On the death of Ignatius, in 877, Photius again became Patriarch. During this latter period of his life—up to 866 when the Emperor deposed him for a second time—the schism was not renewed, but the crisis between East and West was not at an end. Agreement continued to be precarious. Photius had drawn up a list of disputed questions comprising the western practice of fasting on Saturday, the eating of milk foods during the first week of Lent, ecclesiastical celibacy, confirmation reserved to bishops and, above all, the doctrine that the Holy Spirit proceeds, not from the Father alone, as Photius held, but from the Father and the Son (*Filioque*).

During the patriarchate of Michael Cerularius, who came to power in 1042, these various complaints were revived in the East. A man of imperious and ambitious character, he was resolved not to recognize any jurisdiction as superior to his own, and to break with the Holy See rather than yield to it. Through his efforts, writings against the Latins spread through the East, treating them as ignorant people, half Jews and half pagans. Above all, the Latins were attacked for using unleavened bread in the Eucharist, the Saturday fast, eating unbled meat, suppressing *Alleluia* during Lent, ecclesiastical celibacy and the *Filioque* clause, which was considered a heresy.

The ground once prepared, Michael Cerularius struck a tremendous blow. In 1053 he abruptly ordered that all the Latin churches in Constantinople should be closed, and demanded that the Latin monks should abandon the Roman usages and conform to Greek customs. Naturally the pope—who was St Leo IX (1049–54)—protested vigorously. He had a lengthy document drawn up in reply by Cardinal Humbert de Moyenmoutier. Then he sent this cardinal in person to Constantinople at the head of a legation to discuss the questions at issue. The uncompromising attitude of Cardinal Humbert encountered haughty resistance on the part of Michael Cerularius and they quickly came to mutual excommunications. On July 16th, 1054, the papal Legates laid their decree on the altar of Santa Sophia. It was in no way directed against the Byzantine Church, but only against the patriarch and his followers. Four days later, on July 20th, 1054, the patriarch and his Synod replied by excommunicating the Legates, their verdict and their colleagues, but in no way the Roman Church or the pope.

In spite of these reciprocal precautions, this was the beginning of the definitive breach, yet on neither side, however, had one been envisaged. Personal questions aggravated the issues of principle in disastrous fashion. It seems that Cardinal Humbert, who gave no sign of either patience or skill, and showed himself as little like a diplomat as possible, was equally to be blamed with Michael Cerularius, who was quick to take the advantage offered by the clumsiness of the Legate as an opportunity to exacerbate the conflict. Yet the questions at issue were so far from being decisive that on two occasions, in 1274 and again in 1439, the two Churches might have been reunited. Unfortunately, circumstances, and above all Eastern prejudices against the Latins, prevented this reconciliation from enduring.

Is there any sincere Christian who is not deeply distressed by such a separation, whose mind and soul are not constantly tormented by this dismemberment of Christ's flock? The ways of Providence are mysterious. Who knows whether the terrible spiritual ordeal through which the East has passed will not contribute one day towards the rallying of all Christians? Will the evolution of the world's affairs allow such divisions to exist between those who confess the same creed? For the most tragic aspect of this breach between Rome and the Eastern Church—but also that most charged with hope—is that the fundamental truths of our common faith are not in question. And this is the whole difference—but a capital one—between what divides the Catholics from the Orthodox on the one hand and the Catholics from the various Protestant sects on the other.

In conclusion we quote once more from Fr Congar:

> The time of political machinations behind the scenes may be considered as past. That of the "estrangement" is with us still.

Has everything possible yet been done on both sides to help us to understand and to love, to be loved and be understood? The advances made to Eastern Christians by Catholics in modern times seem to be filled with a sincere desire to respect the rites of the Eastern Churches. The documents promising this respect to Eastern Christians, and enjoining it upon Latin Christians, are very numerous, especially during the last century. The papacy seems to have envisaged the problem of reunion as that of a twofold and reciprocal recognition: by the papacy of the rites and ecumenical characteristics of the Eastern Churches, and by the Eastern Churches of the traditional primacy of the Roman See. From the Roman side it seems as though everything might be summed up thus: we respect, and will continue to respect, your rites and discipline, you can have no reason for still standing apart. On the Eastern side there must be a movement towards what is irreversible in the development of an ecclesiology of the Church and the fact of the primacy—not necessarily in all the forms which history has made it take, or even in all those forms which it still presents today, for some of these things are of a relative order, purely historical, but in that minimum which is compatible with a local ecclesiastical autonomy; a minimum such as Photius admitted under Nicholas I, the Bulgarians under Innocent III, and which Innocent IV found the Greeks also ready to accept. This would mean bringing a protracted ecclesiological, biblical and historical labour to a happy conclusion.

Where the West and Rome are concerned, everything comes back to a real acceptance of the existence of the East with its mentality or genius, its temperament, history and the right it possesses of being known and accepted for what it is.

The Protestant Revolution—for it *was* a revolution—which set ablaze the beginning of the sixteenth century, is quite different in nature and significance from the Eastern Schism. The Eastern Schism separated the Eastern Churches from Rome. It broke the unity of Christian discipline, as it had been established by Peter, the Man-Rock, and as it had been maintained by the Church and those who guided her, against all the odds, in the difficult first beginnings of Christianity. Luther, and later Calvin, while remaining faithful to their belief in Christ, challenged the teaching of the Church, on which her tradition is based. It is Christian dogma, and the authority of the Church, that are the object of the attacks of Protestantism. It is the traditional interpretation of the Scriptures that is contested and overthrown. Protestantism claims to go back to the Gospels, but accepting no more than the letter. It destroys the hierarchical order founded by the Church on the primacy of Peter and the Roman See. It brings the Christian soul back to a direct dialogue with its Creator. In short, it opposes to Rome's corporate and hierarchical tradition a conception of Christianity that is both highly individualist and libertarian. These are the two poles of the Christian world.

This revolution had its origins in the past. Although it broke out in 1517 with the publication of the famous theses of the monk Martin Luther on indulgences, many causes had been preparing the way for it for a long time. The two principal causes may be mentioned here.

Firstly, the decline in the prestige of the papacy led in Luther, Zwingli, Calvin and their followers to a genuine hatred of Rome. This had begun with the humiliation of Agnani. For its part, the "Babylonian captivity", as the popes' over-extended stay in Avignon was called, helped to prepare the way for the Great Schism, the conflict between council and the pope, that sombre period during which the Church was divided between two and even three factions.

The second cause was the corruption—and the word has to be used—into which the Roman Curia had fallen; corruption in every sense of the word, carnal as well as intellectual. It may be granted that it would be wrong to see these facts apart from the habits of the times or to judge them entirely by today's standards, but it cannot be denied that, if Renaissance Rome was in full harmony with art, she was no longer in harmony with Christian morals. No Catholic worthy of the name would seek to lighten the shadows of this period. They serve only to emphasize the brightness of the change which was to come.

Reaction against such evil ways led Protestantism into a kind of mystical individualism which took the place of obedience to the supreme Magisterium of the Church, creating to this end the dogma of justification by faith alone and bringing about also the "recourse to the Bible". If I may put it so, the Scriptures became the pope. But the Bible, freely opened to examination, became a cause not of unity but of dispersal. Anyone could put upon it whatever interpretation suited his own ideas. As a result, the Protestant sects multiplied indefinitely.

There are higher reasons for the Protestant denial of the Church's authority that must be given. It represents an intellectual attitude which undoubtedly characterizes minds of a certain stamp. It is a question of two temperaments, two ways of looking at things. André Siegfried, one of the most distinguished minds of our times and well known as a Protestant, in the address delivered before the Académie Française on March 22nd, 1956, welcoming Daniel-Rops, spoke these words:

> I do not think that the true cause of the schism was the scandals in the fifteenth-century Church, for it was not against the perverted Church of the Borgias that the real protest was made, but rather, wha tis far more serious, against the very conception of a Church holding her authority by a transmitted delegation. If the truth be told, throughout that sequence of centuries, obscure or brilliant, during which the rôle of the Church was so great, virtual protestantism always existed in a latent form.

"What is far more serious," writes André Siegfried in parenthesis. How right he is! The depraved manners of the Christian Renaissance are an historical episode. They are related to the miserable condition of mankind, and have only an accidental significance. They are so far contrary to the idea we have today of the papacy that they are no longer imaginable. So it has been for four centuries; for that debased period was only of very brief duration. But the intellectual, spiritual and social impulses of Protestantism remain unchanged. If they no longer apply to the same forms, they apply to the same substance. They are bound up with a particular stamp of mind.

To these principal causes of the Protestant Revolution other accessory and connected causes may be added—the rapid spread of the idea of nationhood, the desire of certain princes to lay hold of the possessions of the Church (monasteries, bishops' palaces, foundations of every kind), the anti-monastic, anti-liturgical, anti-scholastic currents which became apparent here and there. Neither hatred of Rome, nor the appeal to the Bible, nor the *mystique* of justification by faith alone, would have succeeded in winning such large areas of Christendom had not the princes found their own advantage therein, and had they not been quick to pronounce themselves in favour of principles which accorded so well with their ambitions. In a sense, also, Protestantism was the revenge of the civil state against the spiritual power; of the Empire against the priesthood, the lawyer against the cleric, of the "lay" power, if I may use this expression, against power said to be of divine right. In short, the substitution of the city of modern times for the Augustinian city of God.

So Christ's Church, founded on the Man-Rock and firmly established in Rome, has passed through fearful storms during her fifteen centuries of existence. She has been under the constant threat of heresies. Exposed to persecution during the last two centuries of Roman power, given her freedom by Constantine, only to see the disintegration of the Empire, the barbarian invasions from north and south, the breach between Byzantium and Rome came near a hundred times to destroying her. With Charlemagne, she became the very expression of the new civilization in process of formation and had to face all the hazards that her success entailed. Her exploitation for political purposes proved more dangerous than desertion. She was necessarily obliged to protect her independence. She rose to the pinnacle of her power only to experience grievous reverses. Her reputation was compromised by weaknesses unworthy of her. Already she had lost a large part of her following in the East and this time it was in the West itself that the breach was made. Unhappy Church, at that moment she seemed doomed. The cock had crowed three times. Never had she been so wounded or vulnerable. And precisely at this time came the providential recovery which has continued ever since. For if we Catholics admit without the slightest hesitation that we have no reason to be proud of the Roman Church of the Renaissance, we can at least assert that from the morrow of the Protestant revolution the Catholic reform was to return his Church to Christ.

It would be an historical inaccuracy to maintain that it was only under the pressure of Protestantism that the Catholic Church made her recovery, for reform was already under way when Luther's revolt broke out. It had begun in Spain, with Cardinal Ximenes, during the reign of the Borgia, Alexander VI, when the Roman Curia reached its lowest level. It showed itself in France in the selfless efforts of such men as Jean Standonck, Raulin, Mombaer, well before Luther rebelled. Lefèvre of Etaples himself, who is claimed by both camps, was a true champion of Catholic reform. In Italy holiness had never ceased to diffuse its radiance, even when the pontifical court did not shine in the same way. The reputation for charity and humility of Francis of Paola, for instance, must have been remarkable indeed to have bridged the distance separating the French Court and Calabria, and for Louis XI—superstitious, ill and afraid of death—to summon this hermit to his Court, make a confidant of him, and soon afterwards to die in his arms. St Francis of Paola, the founder of the Minim friars (the name he gave to his disciples is significant), contrasts vividly with everything for which the end of the fifteenth century and the beginning of the sixteenth stand in our eyes. And yet this Francis of Paola was not a myth. He really existed. By reason of his sanctity he won this shining reputation just when the example given by the Roman Curia was not one of virtue.

But even at Rome, the centre of the disorder, reform was set on foot by the Oratory of Divine Love, beginning in 1517, a date, it should be noticed, that exactly coincides with Luther's revolt. The foundation of new orders, at Rome and in Italy, furthered this effort of spiritual renewal: Theatines, Barnabites, Somaschi, Capuchins, Ursulines and Jesuits. Although these orders were used to combat heresy, their origin was not due to the Protestant revolt. The Catholic Church was neither dead nor sleeping, in spite of certain deplorable appearances. She had her saints; and a few stars are enough to show the way through darkness. History must never be over-simplified, divided uncritically into "good" and "evil". Those periods which seem to us the most comforting have their blemishes; and those which most shame us have their virtues. Man remains man, with the clay of which he is made and the soul God gave him.

The papacy had had its day of shame. It made the necessary recovery very quickly and, once the sombre page was turned, played a mighty rôle in the Catholic recovery.

This part was played in three different ways. In the first place, the popes gave their approval and encouragement to the new Orders and Congregations, and contrived to make use of them to combat error and win over new peoples in the missionary countries. Secondly, it was the popes who summoned the Council, at first eagerly demanded but later greatly dreaded by Luther and his followers. The town of Trent was made famous by this Council. It proceeded slowly, calmly, laboriously, victoriously, and it accomplished the true reform of the Church, both in dogma and in discipline (1545–63). Thirdly, the popes adopted the Council's decrees and gave them lasting effectiveness. Without the papacy these decrees would very likely have remained dead letters, like so many others. The Council of the Lateran (1512–17), under Julius II and Leo X, had drawn up a programme of reform, but abuses had continued to flourish. Excellent popes like Adrian VI (1522–3) or Paul IV (1555–9) displayed great zeal, but they achieved only insignificant results because they were neither understood nor followed. On the other hand, Paul III (1534–49) had the honour of promoting the Council, Julius III (1550–5) of continuing to support it, and Pius IV (1559–65), admirably seconded by his nephew Charles Borromeo, of bringing it to a conclusion. The work was grandiose and its fruits incalculable. To apply the decrees of the Council there was Pius V (1566–72), a real saint in the papal throne for the first time in centuries. He was succeeded by such energetic and skilful pontiffs as Gregory XIII (1572–85), Sixtus V (1585–90) and Clement VIII (1592–1605). The Roman catechism was published, the breviary and missal were reformed. Seminaries were gradually to be opened in all dioceses for the training of the clergy. The Roman administration was completely reorganized. Important matters were entrusted to commissions of cardinals called Roman Congregations. The pope sent out ambassadors, known as Apostolic Nuncios, whose duty it was to represent the Roman See and maintain diplomatic relations with Christian courts and states. These were wise and effective measures, intended to preserve Catholic unity intact at a time when growing nationalism was confronting it with fresh perils.

Thus, having come through two crises of exceptional gravity, one threatening the purity of the papacy and consequently its spiritual authority and the other separating a considerable part of Christendom from it, that same papacy, far from being weakened by these ordeals, seemed to derive new strength from them. From the Council of Trent and the reforms which followed it, dates a renewal of the Church which has continued through many other vicissitudes to flower to this day.

Daniel-Rops, in his magnificent work on the Catholic reform, having made a careful study of the Protestant revolt, writes: "As the end of one great period in the Church's history —that of the Renaissance and the Reform—is marked in such a superlative manner by the completion of the basilica of St Peter, so at the same time a new century opens, the seventeenth, in which Catholicism is to know a new and wonderful flowering, in terms quite different from those of the past."[1]

[1] *La Réforme Catholique*, p. 392.

CHAPTER VI

FROM TRENT TO 1870

We now enter a new period in the history of the papacy. It was to last for more than four centuries, ending on February 11th, 1929, the date of the Lateran Treaty, one of the decisive dates of this history. On that day one age came to an end and another began. I said in the introduction to this little book that it was no part of my intention to trace the whole history of the papacy—an undertaking which would be beyond my powers and too great for the limits of this book—nor to conjure up the personalities of the great popes with whom that history is filled. I have simply tried to answer the question, "What is the papacy?" At the point we have reached in this account, I think it unnecessary to enter in detail into the pontificates which have succeeded one another from the time of the Council of Trent until the present day. I shall confine myself to describing the chief difficulties which confronted the popes during those four centuries; the main problems they had to solve; the different trials they endured. This is surely the method which will make for the clearest understanding of the development of the history of the papacy, and make it possible to judge the position it occupies today.

The governing fact in the seventeenth and eighteenth centuries is, I think, the development of absolutism in Europe. Sovereigns, uncontrolled and with no real opposition, were everywhere the masters of their peoples. The logical consequence of this fact was that politics became increasingly secular and self-seeking. The Machiavellian idea ruled in the relations between states. The popes were further and further removed by circumstances from the great international debates. When they protested, their protests were no longer heeded as they had been in the past.

Through persistence, intrigues and intimidation, Catholic sovereigns finally obtained the right of nominating bishops and abbots. More or less open competition among the clergy helped them to undermine papal authority. The prestige of the see of Peter remained brilliant. But its action was constantly thwarted or doomed to failure. This kind of diminution of the papal authority manifested itself in two ways: on the one hand, by the appearance of doctrines favouring national clergies and secular authority—Gallicanism, Febronianism, Josephism—and on the other, in the pressure exerted by civil governments and even local parliaments on the papacy, as for example in the matter of the suppression of the Society of Jesus, or in the interminable struggle against Jansenism.

It has often been claimed that the Church favoured absolutism. This is a somewhat simple view. The facts were more complicated. It is true that the local clergy almost always supported absolute monarchy, against the popes themselves on occasion. But the papacy never abandoned the defence of its prerogatives, and to do this it was forced to defend itself against the absolutist kings, and against the intrusion of civil jurisdiction into the very heart of religious jurisdiction. We should remember the attitude of Innocent XI—whom the Church has just beatified—to the absolute king, Louis XIV. Can we imagine that Clement XIV, at a later date, would have decided on the dissolution of the Society of Jesus unless he had been under considerable pressure from kings who, despite their politics, were very Catholic? Did not Pius VI go in person to Vienna to contest the doctrines of the Emperor Joseph II according to which that sovereign regarded Church affairs as matters of state, arrogating to himself the right to arrange and to change everything in the Church? If there had been a time when the popes claimed possession of the "two swords", and the right to wield them, another time came when it was the absolutist régimes which asserted that they had become masters both of the bodies and souls of their subjects. And this was as true of the Catholic as of the Protestant states.

This transference was serious enough when the doctrine and morality of the states concerned were Christian. It became far more serious when these states gradually became "dechristian-ized", or, more exactly, "laicized", that is, when doctrines and morality freed from the Church's discipline took the place of her traditional teaching. To what a pitch might not this danger grow when the prevailing climate became not only indifferent and sceptical towards the Church, but full of hatred and per-secutions against her?

After the corroding intrigues of the eighteenth century, the spirit of the Encyclopedists, of Voltaire and Rousseau, the papacy had to face the dreadful crisis of the French Revolu-tion. But it was not in France alone—although that country played a dominant rôle at this period in the intellectual and political development of Europe—that the Holy See met with formidable difficulties. It was also in Austria, with Josephism, in Italy with a certain form of Jansenism (Synod of Pistoia, 1786) and with Febronianism in the Germanic countries. Under different forms and with varying violence, it is always on a last analysis the same pattern that emerges. In order to fight against it and to protect the deposit of which they were the guardians, Innocent XI, Benedict XIV, Clement XIII and Pius VI were great defenders of the pontifical sovereignty. But the only way in which they could ensure that defence was by yielding ground under the pressure to which they were subjected. By compari-son with the preceding centuries, on the whole the papacy was in retreat. Amid vicissitudes—and worse trials—it was prepar-ing for a new age.

At the end of the eighteenth century the French Revolution sent a tempest blast over the Church and the papacy. The civil constitution of the clergy, the oath required of the clergy, brought France to the brink of schism. Atheism seemed to be triumphant. The goddess Reason profaned Notre-Dame in Paris. Outside France, rationalism spread, and found resounding propagandists in Kant, Hume and Locke. The missionary effort of the Church was everywhere slowed down to the point of seeming to be abandoned. Superficial minds might have claimed that the knell was beginning to toll for Christianity. But the opposite was true.

On March 21st, 1800, the conclave which met in the Benedictine monastery on the island of San Giorgio at Venice (this was the last conclave held outside Rome) elected as pope a mild and peaceful monk, a man of inquiring mind, unshakeable faith and inflexible character in the performance of the duties placed upon him by his office. He took the name of Pius VII. It is well known by what processes Napoleon Bonaparte, First Consul in France, concluded with him in July, 1801, after negotiations lasting more than a year, a Concordat which was promulgated on April 20th, 1802, and which restored the practice of the Catholic, Apostolic and Roman religion in France, and placed the relations between Church and state on a new basis. This Concordat, signed on the morrow of the French Revolution—itself to a large extent brought about by the intellectual, philosophical and political development of preceding generations—is an event of capital importance in the history of the papacy. The work of a century was as it were reversed. The civil power had attacked the papacy on every side. Gallicanism, Josephism, Febronianism had been used to restrain its authority and to set up a defensive system against it. And now France, scarcely emerged from an unparalleled revolutionary and anti-religious crisis, was trying to set up a new order, and appealed to the pope for help in its construction. This was in a sense restoring to Peter's successor the rôle which had just been denied him. Most of all, it was an attempt to adapt the relations of Church and state to the modern conditions of social life. The worst events are sometimes no more than the blundering consequences of necessary change. If one age came to an end with Pius VI in the prison at Valence, another began with Pius VII and the Concordat of 1801. It was to experience many more shocks, many trials, before finding peace. Indeed, it could never attain peace, for true peace is not something of this world. The fact remains that since the reign of Pius VII the papacy has continued to regain authority. And it was to regain it in the greatest degree and with the greatest effect to the extent that it progressively freed itself from the shackles of the past and fulfilled its spiritual mission exclusively.

Pius VII was the pope who worked for the restoration of Catholicism everywhere; not only in the Catholic countries which had been more or less affected by the French Revolution, but in the Protestant countries too, where the Roman Church had encountered the greatest difficulties. In particular he established the Catholic hierarchy in America. The policy of making Concordats which was to be extended so widely in later pontificates dates from his pontificate—after the 1801 Concordat with France. It was a policy clearly indicating the stage the Church had reached. After a period of conflict caused by the rise of nation-states and their intrusive or destructive pretensions in regard to the pontifical authority, the need to regulate the relationship was felt on both sides.

The French Revolution was a tragic crisis. Like all excesses, it provoked a reaction. Excesses and reactions never last long. When the swings of a pendulum are too violent, they balance each other and naturally tend towards equilibrium. The nineteenth century and the first half of the twentieth saw the realization of this gradual adjustment. After Pius VII, Leo XII, who had continued the policy of concordats with Holland, Switzerland and several of the German and South American states, Pius VII and Gregory XVI, who had had to deal in France with the case of Lamennais and the campaign of *l'Avenir*, the longest pontificate in history, and one of the most eventful, began on June 21st, 1846, with the election of Pius IX. It was during his reign that, in 1870, there took place a revolution to which a peaceful solution was only found fifty-nine years later. But that revolution brought to an end, in 1870, an age which had lasted more than eleven centuries—the age of the temporal power of the papacy.

It is no part of my plan to tell here the history of the pontificate of Pius IX. Who is not familiar with it already? I shall confine myself to emphasizing the very great difficulties in which circumstances placed him. Pius IX reigned over the Papal States, as past centuries had made them. But those states lay in the centre of the Italian peninsula, itself divided into states, and the movement for unification which had been growing for the past half century was leading irresistibly to its achievement. Pius IX was a man of great generosity, of ardent faith, overflowing with goodwill, filled with the desire to reconcile, to unite, and to cause the peace of Christ to reign everywhere. He succeeded Gregory XVI, a severe pope. From the moment of the accession of the new pontiff a legend was born. Pius IX was made to appear as the champion of Italian unity. Because, with his generous heart, he had uttered words showing a deep understanding of Italian nationalist aspirations, as early as 1847 there was a widespread belief that the pope would become the leader of the revolutionary movement which would sanction the coming of the Italian State. It was almost expected that the Vicar of Christ would declare war on Austria! There could be no better proof of how the real character of the papacy was misunderstood, even in Italy, its cradle; nor any better proof that the hour of the temporal power had passed.

The pontificate of Pius IX, and its dramatic events—the assassination of the minister Pellegrino-Rossi; the flight to Gaëta; the French intervention; the fighting in 1860; the entry of Italian troops into the Eternal City on September 20th, 1870; the voluntary "exile" in the Vatican—all these are the eventful history of a crisis which was bound to take place, and which, in taking place, was bound to produce many different reactions. It has been said that Pius IX began by being a liberal and ended by being an "integralist"; that he had been to begin with the most liberal pope in history, and became the most reactionary. I do not think that either of these judgements is correct. Or rather, it is not in this simple fashion that the pontificate should be judged. The truth seems to me to be that Pius IX was caught between ineluctable contradictions. The pope could not be expected to bring to an end the sovereignty with which he had been entrusted or to declare war—the ultimate irony—against a Catholic state, in order to gratify the Italian desire for unity. He could not be expected to be a sort of mitred Garibaldi. On the other hand, the Italians could not be expected to forgo their unity—even out of respect for the pope. It was written in history's law of gravity.

All the misunderstandings spring from this. The new principles introduced with violence by the French Revolution had led, as always, to a general reaction in Europe. The Holy Alliance, the legitimist restoration in France—there were so many examples of the reaction. But what there was in those principles that corresponded to the conditions of the modern world—and that was therefore just—was gradually to gain ground, to take shape. The nineteenth century was no more than the progressive and relative application of the excessive ideas of the Revolution. It is a fact that Europe felt the effects of the Revolution after the crisis of 1848 rather than after that of 1789. Italy was no exception to this rule.

The movement of ideas which led to the first attacks on the independence of the Papal States had its inevitable and strong effect on the mind of Pius IX. "I have made a melancholy discovery," he said one day. "The people cannot be trusted." Together with the political movement which threatened an order that had been established for centuries went a process of intellectual dechristianization. The famous encyclical of December 8th, 1864, *Quanta cura*, to which was added the "Syllabus"—that is, the enumeration of contemporary errors —was the voice of the supreme Magisterium calling a halt to the onslaught which threatened Catholic doctrine on all sides. The onslaught no longer had the massive and brutal attraction given it by the revolutionary ideologists, but it was no less

insidious. The defeat of the papal armies at Castelfidardo and
the astonishing success of Ernest Renan's *Life of Jesus* were
two unrelated events, and yet, coming more or less at the same
moment, and both of great significance, they largely explain
the publication of the encyclical *Quanta cura*.

On December 8th, 1869, the pope summoned the Vatican
Council to Rome. This was to proclaim the dogma of papal
infallibility. We shall return to this subject which marks an
essential stage in the history of the papacy. Just when the
Sovereign Pontiff was watching the state on which his power
was established foundering and perhaps about to disappear—
and everything then made Pius IX feel certain that this was no
longer anything more than a question of time—he gained in
spiritual authority what he was about to lose in temporal
authority. Here, in short, was the immense advantage that the
papacy was about to acquire, without as yet even suspecting
it. A few months later, when the troops of General Cadorna
made a breach in the Aurelian wall,[1] they were, without know-
ing it, and certainly without wanting it, giving the papacy the
opportunity to renew its prestige.

[1] This breach was made in the wall which ran along one side of the
garden of the Villa Bonaparte, then the property of the Bonaparte
family. Since 1950 it has been the residence of the French Ambassador
to the Holy See.

FROM 1870 TO THE LATERAN TREATY

Between September 20th, 1870, and February 8th, 1929, there are fifty-nine years. Those fifty-nine years represent the period of preparation during which the papacy was gradually transformed from a power both spiritual and temporal into one that was spiritual only. The personal conduct of the successive popes between the capture of Rome and the Lateran Agreements contributed greatly to this remarkable revival of the authority of the popes.

Pius IX—like Pius VI and Pius VII—had passed through grave times of trial. The end of the pontificate of Pius IX might well have filled with bitterness the heart of a pope who, on ascending the pontifical throne, had felt nothing but generosity, Christian peace and love for his fellow men. The cause of a united Italy set itself up against the Church. In Austria the Concordat was denounced. In Germany the *Kulturkampf* was in full swing. In France, after the shattering blow of the defeat and the vacillations of the new régime, anticlericalism was coming to life again.

"Clericalism—that is the enemy," exclaimed Gambetta; and he foretold the rise of social classes that would be ill-disposed towards the traditional Church. The new pope, elected by the conclave of 1878, who took the name of Leo XIII, saw grounds for anxiety on every hand. He regarded himself as a prisoner in the Vatican. Despite the "Law of Guarantees" voted by the Italian parliament, the position of the papacy was precarious.

The disappearance of the papal sovereignty was generally feared: yet in truth it was about to acquire an even greater brilliance.

Is there any need to portray the personality of Leo XIII, or to remind ourselves of his work and deeds? That pope will leave a shining memory behind him in history. Rightly did the prophecy of the pseudo-Malachy style him, *Lumen in coelo*.

The first of his famous Encyclicals, *Inscrutabili* (April 21st, 1878), announced his pontificate. The new pope declared that the problems that assailed the modern world could only be peaceably resolved by the Christian spirit. He would accordingly devote all his intelligence, faith and genius to resisting the breach which threatened to divide the Church from a part of the modern world. This idea he was to develop in every field. Whether it be in the Encyclical *Aeterni Patris* on philosophy, in *Providentissimus* on Holy Scripture, in *Arcanum* on the family, in *Diuturnum illud* on the state, in *Immortale Dei* on the relations between Church and state, in *Libertas praestantissimum* on civil and political liberties, in *Sapientiae Christianae* on the rights and duties of subjects or in *Rerum novarum* on the condition of the working class, Leo XIII reflected on every aspect of the world and propounded for every problem the solution that was in accordance with both the interest of the individual and of society and the law of Christ.

This perceptiveness on the part of Leo XIII was all the more remarkable—and beneficial—in as much as it manifested itself at the very moment when it would have been dangerous for the Church to refuse to take account of the transformations which were occurring in social life. The attitude of Pius IX was understandable; it was a reaction, natural enough, against developments that were taking place too rapidly. He put a brake on a descent which threatened to degenerate into a headlong fall. It was a cross-roads of history at which a precipitate choice might have been disastrous. Leo XIII approached the situation in masterly fashion. The position adopted by the head of Christendom concerning the working class question will always remain his glory and the honour of the Church.

Great social changes nearly always take place without the knowledge of those who are living at the time. They are brought about gradually, day by day, without anything essential changing in the round of ordinary life. Only at the end of a certain period of time does one realize that a radical transformation has occurred. So it was at the beginning of the nineteenth century, when the introduction of steam power brought about an industrial revolution. In the most highly developed countries, within one or two generations, civilization changed from an almost exclusively agricultural form to an industrial one. Increasingly considerable numbers of the population abandoned their work in the fields and the life of the villages to establish themselves in urban areas where factories were springing up like mushrooms. The clergy failed to realize the significance and the gravity of this migration and did not, therefore, follow their flocks to their new homes. They did not understand—or did not sufficiently understand—that an immense social problem, and consequently a new Christian problem, was about to arise in organizing all this collective and mechanical labour; that a defence of the rights of the human person would have to be formulated from which would emerge new legislation.

It was not the Church alone that was overtaken by these events. Civil government made the same mistakes. Society as a whole showed itself blind. To be surprised at this would be naïve. Man is so made that he lives with his face towards the past rather than the future; force of habit is a vital instinct in him.

I have said that the Church during the nineteenth century had not taken sufficient account of the social revolution brought about by industrialization. I add that Leo XIII was the first really to draw attention to the condition of the working classes for whom the Encyclical *Rerum novarum* heralded a new era. It would be impossible to recapitulate the history of the legislation which has transformed the position of the world of labour without first emphasizing the teaching of this great pope.

The nobility of the mind of Leo XIII, his intelligence and

the genius of his action, could not but yield their fruit. During his pontificate, far from becoming weaker, as might have been expected from the loss of the temporal power, the papacy regained, in another form—and very much more to its advantage —the ground which it had lost.

In Italy anticlericalism ceased to spread and a kind of *modus vivendi* was established between the Vatican and the Quirinal. In Germany the *Kulturkampf* died down. In France, where political strife was still acute and where strong feelings about religion, the sad heritage of the French Revolution, still dominated it, certain principles—amongst them that of the *ralliement*[1]—which later on were to bear fruit—were put forward by Leo XIII.

Despite the bitter attacks to which it was subjected, the Holy See received very notable recognition on the occasion of a disagreement in 1885 between Germany and Spain over the affair of the Caroline and Palos Islands. At the request of the governments of these two countries, Pope Leo XIII played the part of mediator and arbitrator. Abbé Mourret rightly points out that "it is from the pen of Leo XIII, in an Apostolic Letter dated May 5th, 1882, that we find for the first time the expression 'League of Nations', which later on was to become current in juridical language. . . . In 1891, foreseeing future catastrophes, Leo XIII exclaims in his letter *Praeclara gratulationis*, 'We live in a peace more apparent than real. . . . The nations have caught the armaments fever. . . . We must return to the Christian virtues, and above all to justice.' " From 1899 onwards, Leo XIII was supporting the peace conference that opened in that year at The Hague, "in order that it may succeed in resolving disputes between the nations solely with the help of moral forces".

When the Sovereign Pontiff died, at the age of ninety-three —still "a prisoner in the Vatican"—it was agreed on all sides, throughout the civilized world, that in the person of Leo XIII,

---

[1] Leo XIII endeavoured to heal the breach between Catholics and the French republic by encouraging them to "rally" (*ralliement*) to its support. He met with only limited success. [*Trans.*]

Christendom had possessed one of the greatest popes in history. His name will live on through the centuries.

It is a wonderful fact that the political genius of Leo XIII should have been followed by the holiness of St Pius X. At first sight, these two pontificates appear very different. In reality, however, they are complementary and inter-dependent. Leo XIII averted the breach which threatened to estrange the modern world from the papacy. For that world he recalled certain essential truths. Although he concerned himself only with the welfare of souls and the safeguarding of the Faith, his action by the force of circumstances was of the kind that, by simplification, is called "political". The action of St Pius X was essentially spiritual. This is a distinction which, like all definitions of this kind, is not entirely accurate. St Pius X, too, was active at what we have termed the political level; in France the Napoleonic Concordat of 1801 was denounced by the government, the separation of Church and state was voted and the disastrous but temporary rupture in diplomatic relations between the French Republic and the Holy See took place.

Gradually, with the passing of time, the events which characterize a reign or a lifetime assume their true proportions. The reign and life of St Pius X are not marked, save in regard to France, by political vicissitudes. On the contrary, they are penetrated by the influence of the pope on religious life in the purest sense. In this field, St Pius X was the pope of sanctifying grace. To show how this was so, it is enough to enumerate the principal works of his pontificate. They are exceedingly impressive.

To each pope, it seems, Providence assigns his apostolate. The apostolate of St Pius X consisted in renewing the fervour of the priesthood, in reinvigorating its sources, in everywhere revitalizing the purity of Christian faith. His first Encyclical, *Acerbo nimis* (April 15th, 1905), was an appeal to the bishops, the clergy and faithful. The pope denounced the dangers which

assailed Catholic life on all sides; and in the forefront of these
dangers he saw—and with what justification—those of in-
difference and apathy. The Church had more to fear from the
slackness of easy times than from the harshness of persecutions. The formation of the clergy and the quality of the priesthood preoccupied him most of all.

The exhortation to the clergy, *Herrant animo* (August 1908),
is a monument to the glory of the priesthood, as the Encyclical
Communium rerum (April 21st, 1909) is to the glory of the
episcopacy. In indicating the model to which bishops and
priests should aspire, Pius X shows the meaning of these sacred
offices, the responsibility which they entail, and the benefits
which mankind derives from them.

If I may dare to use such an expression, I shall say that it
was a hurricane of purity that the pope sought to unleash
upon society, which the prosperity of the beginning of the
twentieth century was benumbing with materialism. And this
hurricane of purity was not to be limited to rousing the clergy.
It was to arouse all the faithful. St Pius X was the pope who
brought about the greatest increase in the reception of the
essential sacrament, that of the Eucharist. He preached the
Eucharist. He called young children to it. His faith in the all-
powerful efficacy of this sacrament was so ardent that it was
through its reception that he called the Christian world to
regeneration. Such a tremendous reaffirmation of the supernatural, at a time when science was revered as a religion, was
profoundly moving, supremely splendid. It is easy to understand that the halo of sanctity now encircles the head of this
servant of God. One thing is certain. The practice of receiving
the Eucharist has for some considerable time been increasing
amongst the faithful to a remarkable degree, and this is due
in great part to St Pius X.

But St Pius X did not devote his attention only to the essence
of the spiritual life; he concerned himself with everything that
prepares the way for and plays a part in it. Few popes have
carried out more reforms in the life of the Church. The reform
of the breviary, the reform of canon law (an immense task),

the reform of the conclave (so as to prevent a recurrence of the events by which indirectly he had himself been raised to the papacy), the reform of the Roman Curia—all these were his. And it is to St Pius X that we also owe the revival of sacred music.

All this formed part of the activity of a pontificate that was coherent and harmonious but always supernatural. The work of this pope all represents a striving upwards towards heaven. It has been said of him that he had no mind for politics. It is true that the unhappy disputes which brought conflict between the French Government (headed at that time by M. Emile Combes) and the Holy See led to the repudiation of the Concordat, to the separation of Church and State, and to the break between Paris and the Vatican; and it is equally true that the Church in France had to suffer as a result of these unhappy events. But is all that I have just said about St Pius X compatible with what we call in every-day language a political mind? Is this not a question of two quite different worlds? This does not mean that one of those worlds, the one in which human life is lived, should be ignored. Far from it. Everything on this earth has its value, and Christ taught that Caesar had his place. But there exists a hierarchy of duties. The first Christian value is that of faith. The first Christian duty is that of safeguarding it. In preferring sacrifice to compromise, St Pius X may have deprived the Church in France of certain worldly goods. On the other hand, he strengthened her freedom and gave a supernatural quality to her clergy. He ensured that that clergy would possess an incomparable moral authority. It was always purity that mattered for him. *Solvitur in excelsis*: the solution is to be found in what is highest.

It was the same desire for purity that inspired St Pius X in the action which he took against modernism—that is, against a tendentious interpretation of the Scriptures and of the doctrine of the Church. As we saw at the beginning of this book, the Church, ever since her foundation, has had to defend herself against the vagaries of the human mind, against that passion —that noble passion—which makes the intelligence ever seek

to outstrip itself. And Christianity is love, and must be love.
Love of one's neighbour should conquer all vanities. But there
is no lasting victory except through peace. Peace, according to
St Augustine, is the tranquillity of all things in order. The
meaning of true Christianity lies in finding, and holding, the
infinitely delicate balance between what is possible and what
is not—or, more strictly speaking, perhaps, between what is
already possible and what is not yet so; for life is a continuous
creation. St Pius X pronounced on the one hand against a
heresy which threatened the Christian faith in its theological
and exegetical foundations, and on the other hand against a
social doctrine which, although filled with generous intention,
was unquestionably premature: and all that is premature is
false. Does it therefore follow that the pope advocated what
in our modern political jargon we might call "reaction"? It is
enough in reply to such a question to recall the achievements
of his pontificate, of which I have enumerated the various
aspects. If the exhortation to sanctity was "reaction", in what
a heaven should we be living!

The death of St Pius X throws light upon his life, for he
died from the anguish aroused in him by the fratricidal war
of 1914. To the Austrian Ambassador who asked him to bless
the Austro-Hungarian armies which were marching through
the Balkans, the pope replied, "I bless only peace." This sub-
lime reply—as simple as he was himself, and as simple as
holiness—expresses the mind of this pontiff so well that if we
were able to preserve only one of his sayings, this is the one
which humanity should always remember.

Fr Fernessolle and Fr Lethielleux, in their excellent book on
St Pius X, quote two newspaper articles published on his
death. One is an extract from l'Humanité, the paper of Jean
Jaurès, the Socialist; this is what it says: "The pope is dead!
It must be admitted that he was a great pope. His policy was
very simple. It consisted in restoring the values of the faith
with an apostolic steadfastness. He was able to carry out this
policy with authority, thanks to the simplicity of his heart and
the sincerity of his virtue, qualities which have never been in

doubt. From every point of view, if we are to judge him, we must say that he was a great pope."

The other article is by M. Jean Carrère, who was the Rome correspondent of the newspaper *Le Temps*, and who belonged to the Protestant religion:

"Pius X never took any notice of those factors which generally determine human decisions. He always remained on his own ground: the divine. That is why he always sought his only inspiration in his faith; he was a living witness to the reality of the power and sovereignty of the spirit, not fearing to affirm that the Church has all that is necessary to flourish, to fight, to live, and so to remain free and to remain what she is."

Pius X was canonized on May 29th, 1954. That great day was the occasion for an extraordinary manifestation of Catholic faith.

The pontificate of Benedict XV, who succeeded St Pius X, was as it were entombed in the shadows of war. *"Religio depopulata"* was Malachy's prophecy about this pope. What prescience! In fact, it was much more than war that broke out on August 2nd, 1914; it was universal revolution. On August 1st, 1914, an epoch ends; on August 2nd, another begins. Europe, in tearing herself to pieces, brought to an end five centuries of universal sovereignty. The two students of Sarajevo who assassinated the Archduke Franz-Ferdinand threw the world into a succession of convulsions which are far from being ended today.

Benedict XV was sickly in appearance, and delicate in health. Neither his stature nor his voice was imposing. The roar of battle, and that, more deafening still, of inflamed passions, stifled his voice. But few popes have seen the future of Europe and of civilization more clearly. Because of his ability to rise above the violence of the times, and precisely because he exercised supreme magistracy over the universal Church, Benedict XV was suspect to all the belligerents. Each side suspected him of friendliness towards its adversary: the French and the British found him too favourable to the Central Empires; the Italians accused him almost of treason against his own native land; the Germans saw in him their sworn enemy. The pope was attacked on all sides. The truth of the matter is that he tried to keep himself above the tragic conflict. He tried above all to put an end to the war. He saw Europe torn asunder; he saw the powers which had been her strength let loose at each other's throats. He was haunted by the future of our ancient civilization. He measured the dangers arising on all sides, the ravages which this family tragedy would cause in the world as a whole. He made the voice of reason heard. He adjured the adversaries to halt their battles and to agree upon a programme which would take into account the essential claims of the nations which had gone to war to defend the independence of small countries. He offered his good offices, but the interests staked in the war, the passions let loose, the sacrifices already made, were such that appeals to reason received no hearing from either side. Today we must re-read the warnings of Benedict XV in order to appreciate how great a prescience was his, how penetrating was his view, how compelling—but vain—the force of his reasoning. If any man sought to defend Europe against herself, it was Benedict XV. What he realized, before anyone else, was that if the age-old equilibrium in Central Europe was to be totally destroyed, through the breaking up of the Austro-Hungarian Empire, then an immense vacuum would be left in the middle of the old continent, which would unfailingly be filled by a German Reich dominated by the Prussian spirit. And that is exactly what happened. Benedict XV foresaw Adolf Hitler, and was the only man to perceive this danger and, as early as 1917, to warn Christendom against it. To recall the grief which these sombre forebodings aroused in him is the best way to pay tribute to the memory of this pope.

But if Benedict XV was unable to do very much to preserve Europe from its downfall, he never ceased throughout the four years of world conflict in his efforts to ease the lot of the victims of the war. From December 19th, 1914, he entreated the belligerents to exchange their most severely wounded prisoners. On January 11th, 1915, he put forward a proposal for the exchange of various categories of civilian prisoners. In May, 1915, he suggested the internment of sick prisoners in neutral countries—Switzerland or Denmark. In August, 1915, he asked for assurances that Sunday would be a day of rest for all prisoners of war. At the same time he intervened to say that all forms of reprisal should be forbidden without previous announcement of the reasons. In July, 1916, he suggested that prisoners who were fathers of three children and had already served eighteen months in captivity should be sent to neutral territories. In 1916 he requested the Ottoman Government to allow Christian burial to Christian soldiers killed in the Dardanelles. Finally, Benedict XV set up an information agency for prisoners of war which worked from Berne and which, under the auspices of the Vatican, rendered great services to innumerable families on both sides.

The war of 1914–18, during which Italy entered the struggle at the side of France, Britain and the Russia of the Tsars, had found the pope still "a prisoner in the Vatican Palace". The diplomatic missions accredited to him had to be removed to Switzerland, where a representative of the Holy See would come to treat with them. The authority of the papacy was restricted, weakened and impaired by this paradoxical situation. The European conflict gave a new kind of actuality to "the Roman question".

When Pius XI was elected, after the death of Benedict XV, on February 6th, 1922, his first action was to give his blessing *urbi et orbi* from the outer balcony of St Peter's basilica. Since 1870 the loggia where until that time all the popes had appeared, had been closed. Leo XIII, Pius X and Benedict XV, after their election, had each given the first pontifical blessing from the balcony inside the basilica. At their feet they had had only that great church and the faithful who filled it; but Pius XI had at his feet all St Peter's Square, milling with hundreds of thousands of people, and, beyond that square, the whole world.

The new pope's action indicated an idea, a plan, a desire which, during the seventeen years of his pontificate, Pius XI put into effect with remarkable tenacity and logic. The papacy, dispossessed of all its secular power, had lately possessed in Leo XIII a political genius, in Pius X a saint, in Benedict XV a harbinger. In Pius XI it was to have a statesman, and one of the most vigorous in its history.

Five main works mark this pontificate. This statement alone shows its greatness. Pius XI was the pope who founded Catholic Action, which in almost all countries has taken on a decisive importance in the development of the Church. He was the pope who gave a special impetus to missionary work—he almost doubled the number of ecclesiastical administrative areas in the world, carrying the development of the Church to its greatest point. He was the pope who condemned all pagan ideologies, whatever they might be; who vehemently inveighed against the paganism of Hitler's National-Socialism and the persecuting paganism of atheistic Communism. He was, finally, the pope who, working methodically for the establishment of juridical relations between Church and state, concluded a series of Concordats with Latvia, Bavaria, Poland (where he had been a nuncio), Lithuania, Czechoslovakia, Rumania, Prussia, the State of Baden, Austria, and the German Reich. Diplomatic relations between France and the Holy See resumed their normal course during his reign.

Lastly, and above all, Pius XI was the pope who found an honourable solution to the Roman Question. On February 11th, 1929, the Cardinal Secretary of State and the head of the Italian Government signed, in the Lateran Palace, the agreement by the terms of which the Vatican City State was created, all outstanding problems between Italy and the Holy See were solved, and a Concordat between these two powers was established.

Pius IX had lost the Papal States, their capital and the temporal power attached to their sovereignty, on September

20th, 1870. After fifty-nine years, Pius XI placed the papacy on new foundations. One age had lasted almost twelve centuries; another age was beginning.

February 11th, 1929, marks one of the principal dates in the history of the papacy, one of its essential turning points. And this is why it was a providential turning point.

I know very well what bitterness the Roman Question aroused. Not light-heartedly could the break with past centuries that had meant so much for Christian civilization, and for civilization in general, be admitted. Not to understand the reactions that would have been aroused among contemporaries in the event of a renunciation by the papacy of its temporal power would be to be wholly unaware of human psychology: or rather, it would be to judge past events with the mentality of today, which is the worst error that can be committed in making historical judgements. Truth and error, as Pascal said, are not just a question of mountains; they are also a question of time. When the Vicomte de la Guéronnière (who was the brother of my maternal grandfather) wrote, at the prompting of Napoleon III, one of whose intimates he was, the famous pamphlets which foretold the Lateran Agreements, three-quarters of a century in advance, they caused a scandal; and scandal at that time was natural. I repeat: all that is premature is false. Time had to pass before people could realize not only that the papacy would have nothing to lose by denouncing its ancient states, its ancient power, but that it would have everything to gain thereby.

Try to think what would have become of the administration of the Papal States in the modern world! It is not even imaginable.

However, the spiritual sovereignty of the pope could not dispense with material sovereignty. Even if he were treated with quite exceptional respect, the pope could not be the subject of any man. His attendants and advisers could not be anything but his subjects. The Sovereign Pontiff had to be a sovereign. He had to reside on territory that should be his alone, and he had to receive, at the international level, all the attributes of sovereignty.

The creation of the Vatican City State has been the perfect answer to this necessity. What does it matter if it is extremely small—covering only just over a hundred acres? Pius XI said: "The papacy needs only a trunk." That trunk, which raises it above the earth, it possessed from that time.

The Vatican City State is recognized by all other states. The pope is its sovereign. It has its own postal service, radio station and stamps; it mints its own coinage (this is a power more theoretical than real, although there are Vatican coins in circulation). It possesses a railway station, a terminus at which goods trains regularly arrive. The Holy See has the right to send and receive diplomatic envoys. It accredits nuncios and internuncios to foreign governments, and ambassadors and ministers are accredited to it. This representation has developed considerably, in spite of the fact that some countries traditionally represented at the Vatican no longer maintain official missions there. At the beginning of this century there were twenty diplomatic missions at the Holy See; there are now forty-seven—thirty embassies and seventeen legations.

Let us glance briefly across those twenty centuries which separate the fragile beginnings of St Peter's see and the creation of the Vatican City State.

Those twenty centuries appear as a slow and methodical preparation for that event; through so much hesitation and groping—or what seem to ephemeral creatures like us as hesitation and groping—supernatural guidance has been leading the papacy to the position for which it was destined. We have seen the papacy working, in its beginnings, under modest, obscure and unstable circumstances. It acquired stability. It constantly asserted its authority. It projected its authority over the Mediterranean basin, and as far as the limits of the Empire. It was obliged, to a great extent, to substitute itself for that crumbling Empire; to resist paganism, old and new, the intellectual system of the Greek philosophers, the later Judaism. It was made flesh, if one may put it so, because the general circumstances demanded that incarnation. But its true kingdom was not of this world, and to exercise the plenitude of its spiritual office it had to avoid those social forms and to find a position which transcended them.

Gradually, as the nations themselves developed, their development brought about the conditions which gave the papacy its full stature. If affairs are regarded only under their trivial aspect, or, more exactly, in the light of the passing hour, it might be thought that the development of the power of states was a direct consequence of the diminution of the papacy. We have seen this apparent contrast developing between the pontificate of Boniface VIII and that of Pius IX, through the times of Innocent XI and Pius VI. At Savona, at Gaëta, at the Porta Pia, how far we are from Canossa! That is true, but it is only an historical truth. It is not a philosophical truth. In a manner both blind and deaf—and very often it is thus that men proceed, ignorant of the force which moves them—the social and political evolution which appeared to be working against the papacy opened up the way for it. For the prestige of the papacy is not measured by the number of square miles of a temporal domain. It is measured by its universality. It is not measured by its material power. It is measured by its spiritual power.

CHAPTER VIII

THE CONTEMPORARY PAPACY

More than three million pilgrims of all nationalities and all races made their way to Rome during the Holy Year of 1950; in the Holy Year of 1900 there were only 300,000, and in 1925, 582,000.

Most of these pilgrims—and especially all those who came long distances—in a sense "discovered" the papacy. In a disjointed world, rent by opposing forces, they came to understand better than before what the unity of a spiritual society which has existed for twenty centuries and has brotherly harmony as its earthly principle should mean. The opinions and comments constantly to be heard from the lips of these visitors were striking and unanimous in this respect. As in a flash, they came to realize what is meant by the plenitude of the high office of the papacy. To this I can testify.

That office is in fact complex in its nature. To understand all that it comprises it is perhaps necessary to live for some time in Rome, and little by little to realize all that is contained in the history of that capital of the Christian world and remains so miraculously alive today. Then will it be seen that there are in the papal office, if I may put it so, ten distinct elements. Let us try to define them, and then to show their significance.

1. According to the Catholic faith the pope is the Vicar of Jesus Christ on earth; that is, the 258th successor of St Peter, the Prince of the Apostles. We have seen in the first part of

this small book on what facts, traditions and texts we Catholics base this conviction.

2. The pope is the Bishop of Rome, and it is precisely because he is the Bishop of Rome—that is, the head of the Church of Rome—that he exercises supreme magistracy over the whole Catholic Church. It is to be observed in this connection that the Sacred College which elects the pope is composed of seventy cardinals, and that each of these cardinals is either one of the six titular bishops of the suburbicarian sees of Rome, or one of the priests of the fifty-eight parishes which composed the ancient diocese of Rome, or one of the deacons of those parishes. The pope, then, is still elected by the senior clergy of Rome. It is, I repeat, as head of the Church of Rome that he is pope.

3. The pope is the head of that immense international society called the Catholic Apostolic and Roman Church, spread—unevenly—through the five continents of the world and including about 472 million members, as well as a highly-organized ecclesiastical hierarchy. He alone has the power to "feed" this flock; to rule and govern this Church.

4. The pope is the head of the clergy of the Catholic Church, which comprises seventy cardinals, ten resident patriarchs, five titular patriarchs, 307 resident metropolitan archbishops, 42 resident archbishops who are not metropolitans, 1,232 resident bishops, 883 titular archbishops and bishops, 79 prelates and abbots nullius, twelve apostolic administrators, nineteen prelates of Eastern rite, 206 vicars apostolic, 122 prefects apostolic, seven missions *sui juris*, 365,000 priests, one million nuns, and about 270,000 male religious.

5. The pope is the guardian of the deposit of Catholic faith and of revelation, a deposit which enshrines the sacred books of the Old and New Testaments and a tradition which has been handed down from generation to generation until today.

6. The pope is the supreme Doctor of the Church. When he speaks *ex cathedra*—that is when in his capacity as Shepherd and Teacher of all Christians he defines a doctrine concerning faith or morals—he is infallible, which means that the defini-

tions of the Sovereign Pontiff are unchangeable. (We shall return to this later, and will examine more closely this supreme attribute of the pontifical power which, having been the object of passionate controversy for centuries, was solemnly defined by the Vatican Council.)

7. The pope is a sovereign. He reigns over a state that is recognized by all states. It is worth observing that even the Soviet Union recognizes him to be a head of state. We had proof of this in the *démarche* made in 1956 by the *Chargé d'Affaires* of the Soviet Embassy in Italy, to the Apostolic Nuncio in Italy. The Soviet *Chargé d'Affaires* was instructed by his government to communicate to the Holy See—and for this he made use of the services of the Nuncio in Italy as an intermediary—certain documents concerning proposals for disarmament; and it was specified that this *démarche* should be made to the pope as Head of the State of the Vatican City. As I have already indicated, the sovereignty of the pope is illustrated by various facts, among which is the presence of forty-seven foreign diplomatic missions at the Holy See. The pope, by the very nature of his sovereignty, holds a rank apart among the heads of states whether they be monarchs or presidents of republics. He receives their ceremonial visits, and does not return such honours except through a cardinal.

8. Historically, the pope is the heir of the Roman Pontiffs, and this title covers both the old Roman Empire and the Christian era. By a gradual substitution which came about after the time of Constantine, the papacy—we have already seen this briefly—little by little filled the gaps caused by the decline and fall of the Empire. After the darkness of the barbarian invasions, a Christian Rome arose from the ashes of pagan Rome. In a certain sense it was the pope who became the head of this new empire. This historic power is shown in numerous rites and in the splendour of many monuments.

9. The pope—or rather the papacy—is the crucible where spiritual currents from the Hebrew, Asian, Egyptian, Greek, Celtic and German worlds meet and are re-formed. What we call the Roman Church is a fusion of these diverse spiritualities,

reduced to their very essence and condensed and clarified by the Latin genius.

10. The pope, then, if I may put it this way, is a keystone. The papacy commands and upholds an enormous structure; one that is and must be the most many-sided that exists. Is it possible to imagine, despite the unity of Catholic faith and discipline, moods and temperaments more different than those of the Church in France, Spain, the United States, Britain, Latin America, Ireland and so on? Nevertheless, all these Churches form but one single Church. They march together, so to speak, keeping in step. They are sheep of the same flock, and the pope is their only shepherd. It is in him that the unity of the Catholic Apostolic and Roman Church is expressed, which is the greatest strength of the Church.

Such are, I believe, the various aspects or traditions of the supreme Magisterium of the Church, and it is impossible to separate them. One cannot grasp the traditional rôle of the papacy, the reality that is both Roman and universal, without admitting each one of its sources, and their fusion. Anyone who took into account only one of these aspects, traditions or sources would make a grave error. It is this that sometimes makes the supreme Magisterium difficult to grasp for those who are only mindful of its purely evangelical side. On the other hand, when these various elements are brought together, and when it is understood that they are commanded and ordered, then all that the office of the papacy entails, that of a lord and that of a servant, with its abstractions and realities, spiritual heights and temporal commitments, purity and pomp, gentleness and inflexibility, authority and prudence, its "Romanity" and its universality, can be judged.

Confusedly but profoundly the pilgrims who came to Rome during the Holy Year, and took part in some of the magnificent jubilee celebrations, felt all this. Pilgrims of all languages and races who came to kneel at the tomb of the first Apostle and, after the passage of twenty centuries, before the throne of his successor, gave Rome its highest sense of being the capital of Christendom. When Pius XII appeared he personified the fact of Catholic unity. In this world, torn apart by feverish passions and ideologies, where those who oppose a civilization based on Christian faith use all their strength and tenacity to break such a unity and to undo the bonds which hold it together, the office of the Roman Pontiff assumed a vital significance such as can only be matched by looking far back into history.

On November 26th, 1950, one month before the end of the Holy Year, there took place in St Peter's basilica a great ceremony, and one which was particularly filled with meaning. The Greek or Byzantine rite was followed when, in the presence of the pope, the Melchite Patriarch celebrated and seventeen archbishops and bishops of the Byzantine rite—among them two Russians, a Ukrainian, a Ruthenian and a Greek—concelebrated with him. This unusual Mass not only illustrated the union of the non-dissident Eastern Churches in the See of Peter. The very fact that it was celebrated according to the Byzantine or Greek rite—which differs only very slightly from the Orthodox Russian rite—showed that the unity of the Christian Church in all that part of the world depends only on the question of the supreme authority. The faith, the holy sacrifice of the Mass, the liturgy, are the same. I pen these words in hope.

We return now to one of the essential attributes of the papacy—the question of papal infallibility, as defined by the Vatican Council. This attribute is so unique that it alone would be enough to characterize the papacy; it is its supreme distinguishing mark. It is therefore useful to examine its meaning and its scope. In this way we shall obtain a better idea of what the papal power really is.

The constitution *Pastor aeternus* by which the powers and prerogatives of the pope were specified and dogmatically defined dates from July 18th, 1870—a few weeks before the end of the temporal power. But in no way was this an improvisation of the Vatican Council. Dogmas are not improvised; they are

elaborated. The essential dogma of the Holy Trinity did not
receive its definitive expression until the Council of Nicaea in
325; that of the Divinity of the Holy Ghost until the Council
of Constantinople in 381; that of the supernatural motherhood
of Mary until the Council of Ephesus in 431.

In fact, the constitution *Pastor aeternus* was the settlement
of an ancient problem which had given rise to heated controversy throughout the Catholic world, especially in France during the second half of the seventeenth century and the first half
of the eighteenth. The question of papal infallibility was indeed
one of the elements of Gallicanism, and gave rise to one of the
four paragraphs of the famous "Declaration of the Clergy" of
1682, to which Bossuet contributed.

What I have tried to show in this study is essentially the
primacy of Peter in action, through the heads of the Church
of Rome, the popes, his successors. That primacy had been
solemnly proclaimed at the Council of Florence in 1438, while
the conciliar theories professed at Basle were threatening the
traditional teaching about it. And the decree of the Council
of Florence was all the more remarkable for the fact that the
two Churches, of the West and of the East, united then for the
last time, both took part. "We define", declared the Council,
"that the apostolic Holy See and the Roman Pontiff possess
the primacy over the whole world; that this same Roman Pontiff is the successor of Peter, Prince of the Apostles; that he is
the true Vicar of Christ, head of the whole Church, Father
and Teacher of all Christians, and that to him was granted by
Jesus Christ, in the person of Peter, the power to feed, rule
and govern the universal Church, as is contained in the acts of
the ecumenical Councils and in the holy canons."

Such a text was already formulated. However, it did not prevent Gallicanism, Febronianism or Josephism from developing
and upholding theses which conspicuously limited the exercise
of the papal primacy. The object of the Vatican Council was
simply to bring these vagaries to an end and to define the plenitude of the papal power in a manner that would be both clear
and final.

That power, it may be said, is the conclusion of a chain of logic. This is how the Vatican Council expresses that chain; it is necessary to read the text carefully, for it is explicit:

> The eternal shepherd and bishop of our souls, in order to confer a perennial character on the saving work of redemption, ordained the building of the Holy Church, in which, as in the abode of the living God, all the faithful should be included by the bond of one same faith and charity. To this end, before he was glorified, he prayed his Father not only for the apostles but also for those who by their word were to believe in him, that they should be one, as the Son himself and the Father are one. Just as he sent out the apostles whom he had chosen from the world, and as he himself had been sent by the Father, so he wished to have shepherds and teachers in his Church even unto the consummation of the world. But in order that the episcopacy itself should be one and indivisible, and so that, by mutual agreement amongst the priests, the whole multitude of believers should be kept in the unity of faith and communion, he established blessed Peter above the other apostles and thus instituted, in him, the principle and the visible and perpetual foundation of both these unities, on the solidity of which the eternal temple will be raised, and the sublimity of the Church destined for heaven will be made safe in the firmness of this faith.

This is indeed the living chain of which we have spoken. And it is also the unity which descends from heaven and forms itself anew, spiritually, upon the earth. God; Christ; his Church; the apostles and their leader; a perpetual line of successors of the apostles; a perpetual line of successors of the chiefs of these apostles, so that the bishops, the successors of the apostles, may be ever united in the person of the pope, the successor of Peter. Such is the organization of the Church of Christ, as he wished it to be, and valid until the end of the world. The cornerstone of this edifice, then, is the papacy Without it there is no unity.

The powers vested in the pope are precisely and exclusively those which are required by his office. What are those powers? They are stated in the texts we have quoted: the powers of the keys, to bind and to loose; the power of the shepherd of sheep and of flocks; the power of confirming the brethren. The Vatican Council, in the first clause of the Constitution *Pastor aeternus*, defines it in these terms: "We therefore teach and declare, following the evidence of the Gospel, that the primacy of jurisdiction over the universal Church of God has been promised and immediately and directly conferred on blessed Peter by Christ our Lord."

Thus the theology of the papal power has as its first dogma the primacy of Peter, a primacy that is not only that of a spokesman nor that of a kind of honorary president of an assembly. It is a matter of a primacy of jurisdiction giving him the right to govern the Church, to bind and to loose. Peter was everywhere her head. His name, "Man-Rock", which Christ conferred on him the first time he saw him remained everywhere with him.

However, the Church was not made for a single generation alone. She was to continue according to Christ's promise, "until the consummation of the world". "What had been instituted by Christ, in Peter, must necessarily last forever in the Church founded on the rock, which shall remain unshakeable until the end of the world." Of necessity, when St Peter died he left heirs to his power. It is an undeniable historical fact that these heirs were the bishops of the city of Rome, which he had evangelized, where he had founded a Church, where he had suffered martyrdom, and where his body had been buried. That is why the Vatican Council said that "whoever ascends this Chair of Peter obtains thereby, in virtue of Christ's institution, the primacy of Peter over the Universal Church". For this reason the faithful of all lands, according to St Irenaeus, whom the Vatican Council quotes, must remain in agreement with the Roman Church, because of her "most powerful principality".

Of what, then, does this primacy of the pope consist? The Vatican Council made no sort of innovation in this regard. It based its finding on the evidence of Scripture, on previous decisions made both by Roman Pontiffs of all times and by the ecumenical Councils, and in particular on the decrees of the

Council of Florence, in 1438. Now from all these texts, which spring from the two great sources of Christian dogma, Scripture and tradition, it emerges that "the Roman Church, by the will of God, possesses primacy over all other ordinary authorities, so that this power of jurisdiction of the Roman Pontiff, which is truly episcopal, is immediate. It follows that all pastors and faithful, of whatever rite or dignity, are bound to the pope, both individually and collectively, in a hierarchical subordination, and are also bound to obedience to him, not only in matters of faith and morals but also in all that concerns the discipline and government of the Church throughout the whole world."

So speaks the Council. It is only by this means, it explains, that the Church of Christ will form one single flock under one single sovereign shepherd.

Yet this supremacy of the pope in no way detracts from the jurisdiction of the bishops, the successors of the apostles, who retain their divine right, and who are the ordinary and immediate shepherds of their respective dioceses.

It is clear that it is in matters of doctrine that the papal primacy must be manifested. Do not the variations of the dissident Churches, which during three centuries have not ceased to multiply, show the absolute necessity of unity of doctrine? The Sovereign Pontiff, in order to exercise his essential duty, must therefore possess all the indispensable means and prerogatives for the maintenance of that unity. It is not to the pope as a private individual that infallibility is promised and accorded, but to the pope as supreme head of the Church. And that is what is meant when we affirm that the pope is infallible when he speaks *ex cathedra*.

The dogmatic definition of this infallibility is, without any doubt, the main achievement of the Vatican Council. Let us weigh each word of this essential text:

> That is why, by attaching ourselves faithfully to the tradition which comes down to us from the origins of the Christian faith, for the glory of God our Saviour, the exaltation of the Catholic religion and the salvation of the peoples, with the approval of

the sacred Council, we teach and define that it is a divinely revealed dogma that the Roman Pontiff, when he speaks *ex cathedra*—that is, when exercising his office as Shepherd and Teacher of all Christians, by virtue of his supreme apostolic authority, he defines a doctrine concerning faith or morals which is to be held by the universal Church—thanks to the divine assistance promised to blessed Peter, he enjoys that infallibility which the divine Redeemer wished to confer on his Church for the definition of doctrines of faith or morals; and therefore the definitions of the same Roman Pontiff are, by themselves and not by virtue of the consent of the Church, irreformable.

There are many mistaken notions of papal infallibility. The adversaries of the Church, or our fellow Christians who are separated from us, freely argue against this dogma while confusing infallibility with sinlessness, with despotism, with self-complacency, with personal infallibility, with omniscience, and so on. A long list of these accusations and suspicions could be made. None of them corresponds to the reality. The reality is much simpler. Papal infallibility embraces the whole of divine revelation, but it is confined to that revelation. The pope can impose nothing beyond what forms part of the deposit of revelation. His mission is to profess it, to teach it, to maintain it and to preserve it. He has an immense task of conservation and exposition. It is not for him to establish new doctrine. The revelation is complete. A dogma is never defined by the pope by or for himself, as a private individual. The pope can only pronounce in the name of the universal Church and for the universal Church. Indeed, the pronouncement of a dogma entails a long and scrupulous preparation. The pope knows, when he makes his pronouncement, that he is in full agreement with the successors of the apostles. When making known his decision, he expresses and, so to speak, sums up their wishes. The principle of unity is manifested thereby in all its fullness and all its power. *They* are *one*.

Such are the extent and limits of the infallibility of the pope. Beyond these boundaries it is clear that the pope cannot exercise his infallibility. It is no less clear that this infallibility can and must be exercised throughout the whole area contained within these boundaries. It must above all draw out all that lies within divine revelation: dogmas that are sometimes termed "new" are nothing other than the making explicit of truths implicitly contained in what has been revealed. An example will help to make this point easier to understand. A dogma which was always explicit within the heart of the Church is that Jesus Christ is the Son of God made man. This implicitly signifies that Mary his mother was the Mother of God. This title was recognized by the Council of Ephesus in 431. The passage of time led the *consensus fidelium* to grasp that there was complete incompatibility between the title Mother of God and the subjection to Satan which original sin means for every man coming into the world. There came, then, a day in 1854, when the pope, in the name of the whole Church, was able to define explicitly what had implicitly been contained in the title of Mother of God—the Immaculate Conception of Mary. This dogma, then, of Mary's Immaculate Conception, which signified her exemption from original sin, contained implicitly, in its turn, her exemption from the consequence of original sin, which is the corruption of the tomb. In defining the assumption of Mary, body and soul, into heaven, Pius XII, in November 1950, did nothing more therefore than to make explicit a dogma that had been admitted implicitly up till then, and to which Catholic liturgy had referred for many centuries.

Thus the primary object of the papal Magisterium is the deposit of faith. In the implicit as well as the explicit sense, this deposit embraces doctrines concerning the mysteries and dogmas; practical laws concerning natural and supernatural morality; the means of sanctification established by Christ, the sacraments above all; the constitution of the Church; liturgical and juridical order.

The secondary object of the papal Magisterium is the conservation, interpretation and maintenance—in the face of errors which may arise—of all that constitutes this primary object. Papal Encyclicals in particular convey to Christian people re-expressions of Catholic teaching in the light of the historical necessities of each age. Everything in the Encyclicals is not infallible; everything, however, is invested with the authority which flows from the papal primacy.

Two orders of facts, then, are to be noticed especially in the exercise of the supreme Magisterium of the Church. On the one hand there are the dogmatic definitions, in which the pope speaks *ex cathedra* and imposes a dogma on the belief of the faithful. On the other hand are the ordinary acts of the Magisterium which do not involve his infallibility, but proceed from the authority attached to the title of Vicar of Jesus Christ.

It is clear that the latter case is much more frequent than the former. It is extremely unusual for the pope to define a new dogma, in the sense we have just explained. The theologians argue whether the canonizations of saints (not beatifications, which in principle are not directed to the universal Church, but to a local Church) should be counted among the decisions *ex cathedra*. On the other hand, everyone agrees that there are unmistakable juridical signs whereby it is possible to tell when the pope intends to speak *ex cathedra*. These signs are the following:

1. He must be concerned with a matter of Christian faith or morals.

2. The pope must use terms that leave his intentions immediately clear.

3. He must address himself to the whole Church, and not to a local Church, or the Churches of one country or region.

4. He must make clear his decision to bind the conscience of all the faithful.

Beyond these exceptional cases, the doctrinal and disciplinary Magisterium of the pope is exercised in a variety of ways. So is it for him to:

1. Pronounce judgement on the theological conclusions drawn from the dogmas; conclusions which are not themselves revealed either implicitly or explicitly, but are deduced rationally and theologically from the truths of faith revealed.

2. To censure by appropriate theological notes opinions, hypotheses or doctrines which are or might be in contradiction with revealed truth, by drawing up lists of condemned propositions, taken from the works of one or several authors.

3. To affirm dogmatic facts which it would be impossible to doubt without endangering the faith: for example, the fact of a papal election, of the ecumenical character of a Council, of the authenticity of a translation of the Bible, such as the Vulgate; the fact of the presence of a specified error in a given book. (On this last point, it is well known that the Jansenists constantly refused to acknowledge the power of the Sovereign Pontiff to judge whether certain errors were in fact contained in the *Augustinus* of Jansenius.)

4. To approve the cultus of a *beatus* or a saint by processes of beatification or canonization.

5. To approve religious Orders and to ensure that their rules conform to the ideal of perfection taught by the Church.

Beyond the sphere of faith strictly speaking and of Christian morals, the sovereign authority of the pope is further manifested in many ways. When, in order to conclude the Concordat of 1801, Pius VII agreed to call for the resignation of all the bishops of France, or to impose it on them, and to redraw the map of the dioceses, he acted in the name of his sovereign primacy. The pope frequently takes such measures in a less spectacular manner, in establishing or reestablishing the hierarchy in mission countries, in creating vicariates apostolic, in dividing up existing vicariates, in deciding upon or altering diocesan borders, in conferring or withdrawing the jurisdiction of a bishop, and so on.

To make known his decisions or his wishes, the pope may use a Bull, an Encyclical, a Motu Proprio, a Brief, an Apostolic Letter, a Consistorial Allocution, or simply the approbation given in general to the Code of Canon Law, or to the decisions of the Roman Congregations or to the decrees of a particular Council.

In each separate case, the jurists and theologians have to discuss the meaning, the scope and the binding character of the words which come from the lips of the successor of St Peter.

If I have spoken at length on the exceptional nature of the powers attached to the supreme Magisterium of the Church, it is because it is important to understand exactly what the pope represents within that Church. Let us, then, examine it.

The Vatican Council, which codified the privilege of infallibility in doctrinal matters and pressed the unity of the Catholic Church to its furthest point, coincided in time with the end of the temporal power of the popes. At the very moment when the papacy was ceasing to reign over a state, over a people, in the political sense of the verb, it carried its spiritual authority to the highest point. It would be inexact to speak of a transference. The papacy already possessed, in substance and tradition, the unique privilege which the Vatican Council proclaimed. But since that Council no controversy, no restriction, no reservation is any longer possible. Such is Catholic discipline. I will not say, therefore, that the character of the papacy has been changed by the end of the temporal power and the position definitively assigned to the papacy by the Lateran Agreements. Such an interpretation would be mistaken. On the other hand, what it *is* possible to say, is that those events accentuated, underlined and, as it were, stylized the spiritual side of that sovereignty. The pope has ceased to be "a monarch like the others", having been relieved of all the weight which burdens monarchy, and especially the contemporary monarchies; and in so relieving him men have restored to the Sovereign Pontiff the fullness of his influence. They could not have done this had they not been, however, unconsciously, the instruments of providence. (It is enough to glance back and recall the life of Rome as it was in the time of Pius IX, before 1870, to realize how immense is the contrast between the ways of life of the papacy yesterday and today.)

Pius IX (it is true that he was a particularly simple pope) moved easily about amid the everyday life of his subjects, coming and going within his capital city. He was constantly to be seen in this or the other church on special feast-days. Sometimes he would walk alone in the streets of Rome. It is said that one day a child who was walking along in front of him dropped a bottle of wine which broke on the pavement. The child was in tears. The pope, who witnessed the incident, at once entered a nearby *trattoria*, bought a litre of wine, and gave it to the boy, who was now overcome with joy. On another occasion the pope encountered in the street a pauper's hearse, with no one following it. He took his place behind it and accompanied the dead and lonely man as far as the cemetery. Such events would be quite inconceivable today. Not, indeed, that the popes who have succeeded one another since Pius IX have been lacking in the same simplicity or the same evangelical spirit. But this simplicity, this charity, which remains unchanging, could no longer be expressed in this kind of way, for the general conditions of the pope's life are no longer the same. For nearly sixty years the popes considered themselves as "prisoners in the Vatican", and this led them wholly to abandon their informal practices. Moreover, ceasing to be "the king" (kings take their walks at will like ordinary private people), they have become exclusively spiritual leaders. The world is on its knees in their presence.

The end of the temporal power has had a further consequence producing similar effects. It has somewhat modified the relations between the sacred college, the Roman Curia and the papacy. When the pope was a temporal monarch, all kinds of temporal problems necessarily confronted him. He had a state to administer, and this involved public services, civil servants and day-to-day business. In the time of Pius IX, before 1870, only fifteen per cent. of the civil servants were ecclesiastics. All the rest were laymen. It follows that those of the curial cardinals to whom, as to ministers, various administrative tasks were entrusted, possessed special powers. The sacred college was a "senate", in a sense much nearer to the lay definition of that word than it is now. From that time onwards the curial cardinals have been concerned only with purely ecclesiastical problems. The sacred college no longer has preoccupations and responsibilities other than the purely ecclesiastical; and, as the pope's power dominates the members of the sacred college, it follows that the authority of that august assembly has been to some degree diminished. It only recovers that power when the papal throne is vacant; for it elects the pope, a prerogative which constitutes, even today, its essential authority. But this authority is only exerted when there is no longer a pope. Once the conclave is over, the pope is everything again.

Thus, the modern world—and this is the statement to which I have been leading up—far from having diminished or limited the papacy, has only given it greater authority, greater prestige.

Did the modern world wish this to happen? It would be paradoxical to imagine so. On the contrary. The evolution of the human mind, of society, has since the seventeenth, eighteenth and nineteenth centuries inclined most definitely towards the opposite result. Everywhere men sought to secularize the state; and doubtless this was, at a certain level, a matter of necessity. The Church is not made to administer the state. But what is wonderful, if one considers these changes at a somewhat higher level, is the realization that, far from damaging the Church (as some of those who had been pressing for change told each other they would do), the changes were balanced by a substantial recovery of papal authority and by a new flowering of the Church. Such are the ways of Providence, which one must never try to reckon with a pocket yard-stick.

The end of the temporal power of the popes has likewise freed the papacy from all kinds of diplomatic considerations with which it no longer has any concern.

When the pope was the monarch of a recognized state, even if that state did not take up much room on the map of the world—or, to put it more simply, in the Italian peninsula—problems and responsibilities continued to confront him which called for a definite policy. Threats might lead him to draw closer to some, to move away from others. Geographical necessities might dictate this or that attitude. The Vatican was forced to have a "policy" in the strictly temporal sense of the word. In fact, for centuries, it put its policy into effect. It played such a part in history that the phrase "the policy of the Vatican" remains in current language. In certain circles all sorts of diplomatic intrigue—more or less underground and more or less Macchiavellian—are attributed to the Secretariat of State, whereas the reality, when one knows it, is far more simple and natural. Even those who did everything to deprive the papacy of its temporal power have not yet come fully to understand that papal authority had changed its character and that it was being exercised in a different way; if I may say so, in an infinitely more "universal" way.

Thus by "disincarnating" itself and by "spiritualizing" its action more and more, the papacy can occupy in the modern world a position that it would have been exceedingly difficult for it to occupy under the conditions of former times. The papacy doubtless resides in the Vatican City, which is situated in Rome. But this is an historical matter; a question of roots, to use a phrase of Pius IX. The papacy is not *bound* to Europe, as it would inevitably be if it still governed a part of the territory of the Italian peninsula. It is not bound to Europe—I mean to Europe alone, and it could not be so. The papacy is essentially catholic; that is, universal. The pope governs all the Catholic Church spread through the five parts of the globe. This universality of the Church has been continually strengthened during the recent pontificates, by practical measures. A Chinese and an Indian Cardinal have joined the Sacred College. A third resides in Mozambique.

The episcopal hierarchy is drawn to a considerable extent from the native clergy of the various races. Despite the Communist upheaval in the Far East, there is a movement there which has not ceased and will not cease to grow. It certainly raises some very delicate issues; it raises problems which are bound to be extremely difficult, especially in regard to the old missionary nations like France, which still retain, here and there, important positions which they cannot abandon without adding to the disorder in the world. All must go forward with wisdom; wisdom is the very condition of their going forward. Nothing is worse, where civilization is at stake, than to press on too quickly.

Thus does the supreme office of the papacy appear in its fullness and its majesty.

We live in a strange epoch. Rarely has the Church known greater difficulties, or seen greater perils mounting before her. Rarely, however, has she enjoyed a greater moral authority. She owes this authority to the transcendental and eternal values which she represents, to the general circumstances of the world.

CHAPTER IX

PIUS XII
(1939–58)

When the result of the ballot was known and when, in the silence of the Sistine Chapel, now become the centre of the world's attention, the Cardinal Dean of the Sacred College, surrounded by the assembled Cardinals, put the question to the pope elect, "Do you accept the result of the election which designates you as Sovereign Pontiff?", it is not difficult to imagine the feelings of the man called upon in that moment to shoulder all the responsibilities of the papacy—the responsibilities, so noble, so vast and so various, which have been indicated during this survey, where some have been briefly analysed.

The hall-mark of the Catholic Church is her unity. She is identified by this unity, faithful in it to Christ's supreme prayer: "It is not only for them that I pray; I pray for those who are to find faith in me through their word; that they may all be one; that they too may be one in us, as thou, Father, art in me, and I in thee" (John 17.20).

In Catholic eyes this unity desired by Christ is embodied in the person of the pope. He is the incarnation of it. When we obey the pope, we obey without any possible doubt the teaching bequeathed by Christ. To recall a comparison which we have already made to illustrate the essential place of the papacy in the Church, the pope is the keystone. It is the pope, and he alone, who holds together this edifice which is at one and the same time unchanging and many-sided. It is unchanging because its various elements profess the same faith and are subject to the same discipline. It is many-sided because composed of faithful belonging to all the nations and races scattered through the world. This human diversity naturally presents its special psychological problems. It is the pope's duty, therefore, to unite these Churches in one single Church and to ensure that that unity is maintained, while making room so far as possible for local characteristics. This is a supreme task, fraught with countless special problems requiring constant attention. The Holy See brings a vast experience to this task. It is perhaps necessary to have lived in Rome to appreciate the true scale of this Magisterium. Every national Church has a natural tendency to see only itself—that is, to judge wider issues from its own particular standpoint. The papacy, however, sees and must see only the unity which these Churches represent. The levels at which the Churches on the one hand and the papacy on the other function are different and must be so. This truth must be fully grasped if the real meaning of the papacy is to be understood.

Another of these aspects, and not the least significant, can only really be appreciated in Rome. This is what may be called the function of the Eternal City as a meeting-place. The missions which the Church has established in all parts of the world, especially since the sixteenth century, have their centre in Rome, the seat of the papacy. There are in Rome about 1,200 mother-houses or procuratorships of the religious congregations of men and women whose members are spread in large numbers throughout the world. Thus all kinds of questions are submitted daily to Rome by the missions, and Rome replies daily to these questions to resolve them. Rome may be likened to a heart which is continually drawing in and pumping out the blood of the organism of which it is both the motive power and the regulator. Here is yet another proof of the unifying function of the papacy. For Rome is the papacy.

Is there any need to repeat that we are living in a disordered world? Communism, which has such an influence in the world, is essentially atheistic. But Communism is itself a sort of

Church which seeks to substitute the cult of Man for the worship of God. As a first step towards more successfully achieving its purpose, Communism seeks to undermine the discipline of the Catholic Church. It seeks to create disharmony where the greatest human unselfishness is to be found; to exploit misery and difficulties so as to use them against the discipline of the Catholic Church. Communist tactics make use of every kind of trick, so successfully that some Catholics, brimming over with good faith and carried away by the logic of their ideal, sometimes allow themselves to make common cause with the Communists, convinced that they are being faithful to their creed, and even convinced that they alone are faithful to it. Atheistic Communism goes to any length, therefore, to attract these well-meaning souls in this way, to flatter them, to promise them alliances, pay, profits and, when the break with Rome is complete, passes to the second stage of its programme, that of de-Christianization. For there is no possible basis of agreement between Communist doctrine and Christianity. The one excludes the other. If there were any possibility of agreement, it would mean either that Communism was no longer conforming to Communist doctrine or that Catholicism was no longer conforming to the doctrine of the Church. But there is no doubt that there has been a danger of serious indiscipline along these lines. It is the business of the papacy to guard against this danger, and to combat it with all the means at its disposal. Here the papacy is seen in its historical rôle, as it has fulfilled it for the past two thousand years. If the Catholic Church is what she is, it is because the papacy has always fulfilled this pastoral mission. The Lord still says, "Simon, Simon, behold Satan has claimed power over you all, so that he can sift you like wheat: but I have prayed for thee, that thy faith may not fail; when, after a while, thou hast come back to me, it is for thee to be the support of thy brethren." (Luke 26.31.)

The pope is guardian of the deposit of Faith, guardian of Catholic unity, supreme Doctor, supreme Magistrate, supreme

Arbiter, heart of the Universal Church. And Pope Pius XII possessed an active conception of the range of this position and the responsibilities which it involves. To banish any doubt about this it is enough to glance through the sixteen volumes containing the Encyclicals, Apostolic Letters, Discourses, radio messages, Allocutions published during his pontificate. For he was an indefatigable worker, whose capacity for work almost passed belief. It may be said that not a single matter affecting the life of the Church escaped the notice of Pius XII; that there was not a single subject on which he did not express his views. For everything is in all. God is everywhere. The soul is in everything. There is no task here on earth, however humble or tedious it may be, which cannot be related to the infinite. Pius XII set himself to expound this truth. His priestly work was a kind of encyclopedia: but an encyclopedia in God.

A long career, during which he had been constantly studying the varied problems of this world, prepared Cardinal Pacelli for his pontifical mission. But it may be said that he conceived that mission on the grandest scale. The personality of Pius XII was such that it did much to increase the influence of the papacy abroad.

Physically, Pius XII was a tall, thin man, who looked frail, but whose fragility was that of steel. He had an indomitable energy. He had a rather small head, a Roman nose, a face in which the bones were prominent. He was pale, and often sallow. Behind his gold-rimmed spectacles two dark eyes looked out—I was going to say looked through you—with an extraordinary brightness. He had long and noble hands. His courtesy was exemplary. One immediately felt at ease in his presence. A visitor entered his room almost trembling with emotion, but at once found himself in the presence of the most welcoming and simple of talkers. Pius XII became very animated in conversation, and a chance remark often made him laugh. His expression was detached and grave when he celebrated the holy sacrifice or when he prayed, but he could be lively when the time was appropriate, and show himself interested in the most unimportant things and in touch with the

world about him. But when he presided at a ceremony in
the Vatican Basilica, when he was seated on the throne of the
Church wearing the pontifical insignia as the rites of the Roman
liturgy were carried out before him, nothing could equal
the grandeur of his person—a grandeur which came from the
reverence with which he fulfilled his sacred function. Each of
his predecessors possessed his own mark of distinction. Leo
XIII, small as he was, impressed with his effulgent genius.
The sanctity of Pius X gave him a halo even in his lifetime. The
gaze of Benedict XV compelled attention for its intelligence.
Pius XI was power personified. But I do not think that
any pope can have been or could be the very incarnation of
the idea of the papacy more than was Pius XII. He possessed
the two supreme qualities of simplicity and majesty.

Occupying a position where it was possible to look out upon
all the world, and to form judgements on the affairs which
were shaking it—judgements not distorted by the problems
which daily seized temporal governments by the throat—Pius
XII, already versed by experience in international affairs,
acceded to the papacy in one of the gravest hours through
which the Church has passed. For the second time, an inhuman
conflict was about to devastate Europe, to tear Christendom
asunder, to shake the foundations of civilization. The order
established for centuries was everywhere about to crumble. A
new era was about to begin. Many nations were suddenly to
be given independence, while others, established for centuries,
were to lose it. The Communist heresy, already spread and
maintained by force in a large part of the world, was to find
very suitable terrain for its progress in this frenzy of emanci-
pation. Nationalism was to become in its turn the opium of
the people. In Europe and Asia, and in certain parts of Africa,
the Catholic Church was to be confronted with these ordeals
and these dangers. She had to find the exact point at which
the realm of Caesar ended and that of God began. In the heart
of the Church itself there was danger of indiscipline, for Communism spreads its influence everywhere and is all the more
perfidious when acting in the name of charity. Firmness, justice,

flexibility, patience, understanding, uprightness, energy, all these virtues and their combination were required to keep the Church on the straight path. And above all the Faith which embraces them all.

In his countless teachings Pope Pius XII never missed an opportunity of appealing to these virtues. A study of the message addressed to all Christians on Christmas Day, 1956, is enough to show that on all problems which beset the nations of the world and on which the Church had a word to say, Pius XII said that word in the way it needed to be said. Moreover, the dignity with which he exercised his Magisterium gave him exceptional authority. That authority was asserted not only in the predominantly Catholic countries, but also in those which are separated from the Roman Church or do not share the Christian faith.

Pius XII died on October 9th, 1958, at the age of eighty-two, after a pontificate of nineteen years and seven months. The conclave for the election of his successor began on October 26th; at the twelfth scrutiny, on October 28th, Cardinal Roncalli was elected and took the name of John XXIII.

Angelo Giuseppe Roncalli, the son of a peasant farmer, was born on November 25th, 1881, at Sotto il Monte, a village forty miles east of Milan in the diocese of Bergamo. He entered the junior seminary at Bergamo at the age of eleven in 1892, took his degree in theology in Rome in 1902 and was ordained priest there in the same year. From 1905 to 1914 he acted as secretary to the Bishop of Bergamo and taught history and patrology in the diocesan seminary. After service with the Italian army during the war of 1914–18, he was appointed in 1921 to the Sacred Congregation de Propaganda Fide. In 1925 began his career in the Vatican diplomatic service with his appointment by Pius XI as Apostolic Visitor to Sofia whence, after ten years, he was transferred to Istanbul as Apostolic Delegate. His work for nineteen years in the Balkans made him an expert in the complicated affairs of that territory. In December 1944 came the most difficult assignment of Mgr Roncalli's career as a papal diplomat; he was appointed

Nuncio in Paris in succession to Cardinal Maglione at a particularly difficult time when, with the collapse of the Vichy régime and the end of the war, many complex problems affecting the relations of the Church with the French Republic emerged. In addition, after 1952, Mgr Roncalli acted as the Holy See's permanent observer at Unesco. At the consistory of January 12th, 1953, Pius XII created him Cardinal priest of the title of St Prisca and three days later named him Patriarch of Venice; this was his office at the time of his election. The coronation of John XXIII took place on November 4th, 1958.

At the end of two thousand years the papacy is more alive than ever. The *Tu es Petrus* applies to the end of time.

CHRONOLOGICAL LIST
OF THE POPES

St PETER, of Bethsaida in Galilee, Prince of the Apostles, who received from Jesus Christ the sovereign power of the pontificate, which he was to transmit to his successors: resided first at Antioch, and then, according to the record dating from 354, for twenty-five years in Rome, where he suffered martyrdom in the year 64 or 67.

St LINUS, 67–76. Up to Eleutherius the years at the beginning and end of the pontificates are not accurate to within a year. Thereafter, until half-way through the eleventh century, there is still some doubt about the month or the day. Two or three dates, month and day, at the beginning of a pontificate in this list indicate the election, the ordination and the coronation. The traditional reckoning of the years of a pontificate began with the coronation.

St ANACLETUS or Cletus, 76–88.

St CLEMENT I, 88–97.

St EVARISTUS, 97–105.

St ALEXANDER I, 105–15.

St SIXTUS I, 115–25.

St TELESPHORUS, 125–36.

St HYGINUS, 136–40.

St PIUS I, 140–55.

St ANICETUS, 155–66.

St SOTER, 166–75.

St ELEUTHERIUS, 175–89.

St VICTOR I, 189–99.

St ZEPHYRINUS, 199–217.

St CALLISTUS I, 217–22.

    [St HIPPOLYTUS, 217–35.]

St URBAN I, 222–30.

St PONTIAN, July 21st, 230–Sept. 28th, 235.

St ANTERUS, Nov. 21st, 235–Jan. 3rd, 236.

St FABIAN, Jan. 10th, 236–Jan. 20th, 250.

St CORNELIUS, March 251–Aug. 2nd, 253.

    [St NOVATIAN, 251.]

St LUCIUS I, June 26th, 253–March 5th, 254.

St STEPHEN I, May 12th, 254–Aug. 2nd, 257.

St SIXTUS II, Aug. 30th, 257–Aug. 6th, 258.

St DIONYSIUS, July 22nd, 259–Dec. 26th, 268.

St FELIX I, Jan. 5th, 269–Dec. 30th, 274.

St EUTYCHIAN, Jan. 4th, 275–Dec. 7th, 283.

St CAIUS, Dec. 17th, 283–April 22nd, 296.

St MARCELLINUS, June 30th, 296–Oct. 25th, 304.

St MARCELLUS I, May 27th (or June 26th), 308–Jan. 16th, 309.

St EUSEBIUS, April 18th, 309–Aug. 17th, 310.

St MELCHIADES, July 2nd, 311–Jan. 11th, 314.

St SILVESTER I, Jan. 31st, 314–Dec. 31st, 335.

St MARK, Jan. 18th, 336–Oct. 10th, 336.

St JULIUS I, Feb. 6th, 337–April 12th, 352.

LIBERIUS, May 17th, 352–Sept. 24th, 366.

[St FELIX II, 355–Nov. 22nd, 365. Confused with a St Felix who was martyred at Rome; became known as St Felix II in the line of the Roman pontiffs, thus causing an error in the numbering of the legitimate popes Felix III and Felix IV and the anti-pope Felix V, who should be known as II, III and IV respectively.]

St DAMASCUS I, Oct. 1st, 366–Dec. 11th, 384.

    [URSICINUS, 366–367.]

St SIRICIUS, Dec. 15th, 22nd or 29th, 384–Nov. 26th, 399.

St ANASTASIUS I, Nov. 27th, 399–Dec. 19th, 401.

St INNOCENT I, Dec. 22nd, 401–March 12th, 417.

St ZOSIMUS, March 18th, 417–Dec. 26th, 418.

St BONIFACE I, Dec. 28th or 29th, 418–Sept. 4th, 422.
[EULALIUS, Dec. 27th or 29th, 418–419.]

St CELESTINE I, Sept. 10th, 422–July 27th, 432.

St SIXTUS III, July 31st, 432–Aug. 19th, 440.

St LEO I, the GREAT, Sept. 29th, 440–Nov. 11th, 461.

St HILARIUS, Nov. 19th, 461–Feb. 2nd, 468.

St SIMPLICIUS, March 3rd, 468–March 10th, 483.

St FELIX III (II), March 13th, 483–March 1st, 492.

St GELASIUS I, March 1st, 492–Nov. 21st, 496.

ANASTASIUS II, Nov. 24th, 496–Nov. 19th, 498.

St SYMMACHUS, Nov. 22nd, 498–July 19th, 514.
[LAWRENCE, 498–501–505.]

St HORMISDAS, July 20th, 514–July 6th, 523.

St JOHN I, Aug. 13th, 523–May 18th, 526.

St FELIX IV (III), July 12th, 526–Sept. 22nd, 530.

BONIFACE II, Sept. 22nd, 530–Oct. 17th, 532.
[DIOSCOROS, Sept. 22nd, 530–Oct. 14th, 530. Dioscoros, who died twenty-two days after his election, was perhaps legitimate.]

JOHN II, Jan. 1st, 533–May 8th, 535.

St AGAPITUS I, May 13th, 535–April 22nd, 536.

St SILVERIUS, June 1st or 8th, 536–Nov. 11th, 537. (Deposed by force in March, apparently resigned on November 11th, and died on December 2nd.)

VIGILIUS, March 29th, 537–June 7th, 555. (Imposed by Belisarius, March 29th, 537; became the legitimate pope as a result of the resignation of St Silverius and with the consent of the clergy of Rome, which thus repaired the deficiency of the election.)

PELAGIUS I, June 16th, 556– March 4th, 561.

JOHN III, July 17th, 561–July 13th, 574.

BENEDICT I, June 2nd, 575–July 30th, 579.

PELAGIUS II, Nov. 26th, 579–Feb. 7th, 590.

St GREGORY I, the GREAT, Sept. 3rd, 590–March 12th, 604.

SABINIAN, Sept. 13th, 604–Feb. 22nd, 606.

BONIFACE III, Feb. 19th, 607–Nov. 12th, 607.

St BONIFACE IV, Aug. 25th, 608–May 8th, 615.

St Deusdedit i (or Adeodatus i), Oct. 19th, 615–Nov. 8th, 618.

Boniface v, Dec. 23rd, 619–Oct. 25th, 625.

Honorius i, Oct. 27th, 625–Oct. 12th, 638.

Severinus, May 28th, 640–Aug. 2nd, 640.

John iv, Dec. 24th, 640–Oct. 12th, 642.

Theodore i, Nov. 24th, 642–May 14th, 649.

St Martin i, July, 649–Sept. 16th, 655.

St Eugenius i, Aug. 10th, 654–June 2nd, 657.

(After St Martin had been arrested and deported, June 17th, 653, his successor was appointed on Aug. 10th, 654, and it appears that St Martin raised no objection.)

St Vitalian, July 30th, 657–Jan. 27th, 672.

Deusdedit ii, April 11th, 672–June 17th, 676.

Donus, Nov. 2nd, 676–April 11th, 678.

St Agatho, June 27th, 678–April 10th, 681.

St Leo ii, Aug. 17th, 682–July 3rd, 683.

St Benedict ii, June 26th, 684–May 8th, 685.

John v, July 23rd, 685–Aug. 2nd, 686.

Conon, Oct. 21st, 686–Sept. 21st, 687.

[Theodore, 687.]

[Paschal, 687.]

St Sergius i, Dec. 15th, 687–Sept. 8th, 701.

John vi, Oct. 30th, 701–Jan. 11th, 705.

John vii, March 1st, 705–Oct. 18th, 707.

Sisinnius, Jan. 15th, 708–Feb. 4th, 708.

Constantine, March 25th, 708–April 9th, 715.

St Gregory ii, May 19th, 715–Feb. 11th, 731.

St Gregory iii, March 18th, 731–Nov. 741.

St Zachary, Dec. 10th, 741–March 22nd, 752.

Stephen ii, March 23rd, 752–March 25th, 752.

Stephen iii, March 26th, 752–April 26th, 757.

St Paul i, April 29th, 757–June 28th, 767.

[Constantine, June 28th, July 5th, 767–9.]

[Philip, July 31st, 768. On the very day of his election he returned to his monastery.]

Stephen iv, Aug. 1st, 7th, 768–Jan. 24th, 772.

ADRIAN I, Feb. 1st, 9th, 772–Dec. 25th, 795.

St LEO III, Dec. 27th, 795–June 12th, 816.

St STEPHEN V, June 22nd, 816–Jan. 24th, 817.

St PASCHAL I, Jan. 25th, 817–Feb. 11th, 824.

EUGENIUS II, May 11th, 824–Aug., 827.

VALENTINE, Aug. 827–Sept., 827.

GREGORY IV, 827–Jan., 844.

    [JOHN, Jan., 844.]

SERGIUS II, Jan., 844–Jan. 27th, 847.

St LEO IV, April 1st, 10th, 847–July 17th, 855.

BENEDICT III, Sept. 29th, 855–April 17th, 858.

    [ANASTASIUS, the librarian, Aug., 855–Sept., 855.]

St NICHOLAS I, the Great, April 24th, 858–Nov. 13th, 867.

ADRIAN II, Dec. 14th, 867–Dec. 14th, 872.

JOHN VIII, Dec. 14th, 872–Dec. 16th, 882.

MARINUS I, Dec. 16th, 882–May 15th, 884.

St ADRIAN III, May 17th, 884–Sept., 885.

STEPHEN VI, Sept., 885–Sept. 14th, 891.

FORMOSUS, Oct. 6th, 891–April 4th, 896.

BONIFACE VI, April, 896–April, 896.

STEPHEN VII, May, 896–Aug., 897.

ROMANUS, Aug., 897–Sept., 897.

THEODORE II, Dec., 897–897.

JOHN IX, Jan., 898–Jan. 900.

BENEDICT IV, Feb. 1st, 900–July, 903.

LEO V, July, 903–Sept., 903.

    [CHRISTOPHER (122), Aug. or Sept., 903–Jan., 904.]

SERGIUS III, Jan., 29th, 904–April 14th, 911.

ANASTASIUS III, April, 911–June, 913.

LANDO, July, 913–Feb., 914.

JOHN X, March, 914–May, 928.

LEO VI, May, 928–Dec., 928.

STEPHEN VIII, Dec., 928–Feb., 931.

JOHN XI, March 11th, 931–Dec., 935.

LEO VII, Jan. 8th, 936–July 13th, 939.

STEPHEN IX, July 14th, 939–Oct., 942.

MARINUS II, Oct. 30th, 942–May, 946.

AGAPITUS II, May 10th, 946–Dec., 955.

JOHN XII, Octavian of the Counts of Tusculum, Dec. 16th, 955–May 14th, 964.

LEO VIII, June 4th, 963–March 1st, 965.

BENEDICT V, May 22nd, 964–July 4th, 966. (If Leo VIII was the legitimate pope, Benedict V, who was deposed at another Synod held at the Lateran by Leo VIII and the Emperor Otto I on June 23rd, 964, is an anti-pope.)

JOHN XIII, Oct. 1st, 965–Sept. 9th, 972.

BENEDICT VI, Jan. 19th, 973–April, 974.

[In 972 a pope Donus or Doninus II, who never existed, appears in the list.]

[Boniface VII, June–July, 974; then Aug., 984–July, 985.]

BENEDICT VII, Oct., 974–July 10th, 983.

JOHN XIV, Dec., 983–Aug. 20th, 984.

JOHN XV, Aug., 985–March, 996.

GREGORY V, Bruno, of the Dukes of Carinthia, May 3rd, 996–Feb. 18th, 999.

[JOHN XVI, April, 997–Feb. 998.]

SILVESTER II, April 2nd, 999–May 12th, 1003.

JOHN XVII, June, 1003–Dec., 1003.

JOHN XVIII, Jan., 1004–July, 1009.

SERGIUS IV, July 31st, 1009–May 12th, 1012.

BENEDICT VIII, Theophylactus, of the Counts of Tusculum, May 18th, 1012–24.

JOHN XIX, Romanus, of the Counts of Tusculum, April–May, 1024–1032.

BENEDICT IX, Theophylactus, of the Counts of Tusculum, 1032–1044.

SILVESTER III, Jan. 20th, 1045–March 10th, 1045.

[BENEDICT IX (for the second time), April 20th, 1045–May 1st, 1045.]

GREGORY VI, May 5th, 1044–Dec. 20th, 1046.

CLEMENT II, Lord of the Lords of Morsleben and Hornburg, Dec. 24th, 25th, 1046–Oct. 9th, 1047.

[BENEDICT IX (for the third time), Nov. 8th, 1047–July 17th, 1048.]

DAMASUS II, Poppo, July 17th, 1048–Aug. 9th, 1048.

St LEO IX, Bruno, of the Counts of Egisheim-Dagsburg, Feb. 12th, 1049–April 19th, 1054.

VICTOR II, April 16th, 1055–July 28th, 1057.

STEPHEN X, Aug. 3rd, 1057–March 29th, 1058.

[BENEDICT X, April 5th, 1058–Jan. 24th, 1059.]

NICHOLAS II, Jan. 1st, 1059–July 27th, 1061.

ALEXANDER II, Oct. 1st, 1061–April 21st, 1073.

[HONORIUS II, Oct. 10th, 1061–1072.]

St GREGORY VII, April 22nd, June 30th, 1073–May, 25th, 1085.

[CLEMENT III, June 25th, 1080–March 24th, 1084–Sept. 8th, 1100.]

Bd VICTOR III, May 24th, 1086–Sept. 16th, 1087.

Bd URBAN II, March 12th, 1088–July 29th, 1099.

PASCHAL II, Aug. 13th, 14th, 1099–Jan. 21st, 1118.

[THEODORIC, Bishop of Santa Rufino, 1100–1102.]

[ALBERT, Bishop of Sabine, –1102.]

[SILVESTER IV, Nov. 18th, 1103–Jan. 1st, 1111.]

GELASIUS II, Jan. 24th, March 10th, 1118–Jan. 28th, 1119.

[GREGORY VIII, March 8th, 1118–1121.]

CALLISTUS II, Feb. 2nd, 9th, 1119– Dec. 13th, 1124.

HONORIUS II, Dec. 15th, 21st, 1124–Feb. 13th, 1130.

[CELESTINE II, Dec., 1124.]

INNOCENT II, Feb. 14th, 23rd, 1130–Sept. 24th, 1143.

[ANACLETUS II, Feb. 14th, 23rd, 1130–Jan. 25th, 1138.]

[VICTOR IV, March, 1138–May 29th, 1138.]

CELESTINE II, Sept. 26th, Oct. 3rd, 1143–March 8th, 1144.

LUCIUS II, March 12th, 1144–Feb. 15th, 1145.

Bd EUGENIUS III, Feb. 15th, 18th, 1145–July 18th, 1153.

ANASTASIUS IV, July 12th, 1153–Dec. 3rd, 1154.

ADRIAN IV, Dec. 4th, 5th, 1154–Sept. 1st, 1159.

ALEXANDER III, Sept. 7th, 20th, 1159–Aug. 30th, 1181.

[VICTOR IV, Sept. 7th, Oct. 4th, 1159–April 20th, 1164.]

[PASCHAL III, April 22nd, 26th, 1164–Sept. 20th, 1168.]

[CALLISTUS III, Sept., 1168–Aug. 29th, 1178.]

[INNOCENT III, Sept. 29th, 1179–1180.]

LUCIUS III, Sept. 1st, 6th, 1181–Sept. 25th, 1185.

URBAN III, Nov. 25th, Dec. 1st, 1185–Oct. 20th, 1187.

GREGORY VIII, Oct. 21st, 25th, 1187–Dec. 17th, 1187.

CLEMENT III, Dec. 19th, 20th, 1187–March, 1191.

CELESTINE III, March 30th, April 14th, 1191–Jan. 8th, 1198.

INNOCENT III, Jan. 8th, Feb. 22nd, 1198–July 16th, 1216.

HONORIUS III, July 18th, 24th, 1216–March 18th, 1227.

GREGORY IX, March 19th, 21st, 1227–Aug. 22nd, 1241.

CELESTINE IV, Oct. 25th, 28th, 1241–Nov. 10th, 1241.

INNOCENT IV, June 25th, 28th, 1243–Dec. 7th, 1254.

ALEXANDER IV, Dec. 12th, 20th, 1254–May 25th, 1261.

URBAN IV, Aug. 29th, Sept. 4th, 1261–Oct. 2nd, 1264.

CLEMENT IV, Feb. 5th, 15th, 1265–Nov. 29th, 1268.

Bd GREGORY X, Sept. 1st, 1271, March 27th, 1272–Jan. 10th, 1276.

Bd INNOCENT V, Jan. 21st, Feb. 22nd, 1276–June 22nd, 1276.

ADRIAN V, July 7th, 1276–Aug. 18th, 1276.

JOHN XXI, Sept. 8th, 20th, 1276–May 20th, 1277.

> [A pope said to have borne the name of John XX never in fact existed; when after two-and-a-half centuries the name of John was resumed, Peter Ispano who, strictly speaking, was John XIX, took the name of John XXI.]

NICHOLAS III, Nov. 25th, Dec. 26th, 1277–Aug. 22nd, 1280.

MARTIN IV, Feb. 22nd, March 23rd, 1281–March 28th, 1285 (as Marinus I and Marinus II were also known as Martin, the new pope was called Martin IV).

HONORIUS IV, April 2nd, May 20th, 1285–April 3rd, 1287.

NICHOLAS IV, Feb. 22nd, 1288–April 4th, 1292.

St CELESTINE V, July 5th, Aug. 29th, 1294–Dec. 13th, 1294.

BONIFACE VIII, Dec. 24th, 1294, Jan. 23rd, 1295–Oct. 11th, 1303.

Bd BENEDICT XI, Oct. 22nd, 27th, 1303–July 7th, 1304.

CLEMENT V, June 5th, Nov. 14th, 1305–April 20th, 1314.

JOHN XXII, Aug. 7th, Sept. 5th, 1316–Dec. 4th, 1334.

> [NICHOLAS V, May 12th, 22nd, 1328–Aug. 25th, 1330.]

BENEDICT XII, Dec. 20th, 1334, Jan. 8th, 1335–April 25th, 1342.

CLEMENT VI, May 7th, 19th, 1342–Dec. 6th, 1352.

INNOCENT VI, Dec. 18th, 30th, 1352–Sept. 21st, 1362.

Bd URBAN V, Sept. 28th, Nov. 6th, 1362–Dec. 19th, 1370.

GREGORY XI, Dec. 30th, 1370, Jan. 5th, 1371–March 26th, 1378.

URBAN VI, April 8th, 18th, 1378–Oct. 15th, 1389.

BONIFACE IX, Nov. 2nd, 9th, 1389–Oct. 1st, 1404.

INNOCENT VII, Oct 17th, Nov. 11th, 1404–Nov. 6th, 1406.

GREGORY XII, Nov. 30th, Dec. 19th, 1406–July 4th, 1415.

> [CLEMENT VII, Sept. 20th, Oct. 31st, 1378–Sept. 16th, 1394.]

> [BENEDICT XIII, Sept. 28th, Oct. 11th, 1394–May 23rd, 1423.]

> [ALEXANDER V, June 26th, July 7th, 1409–May 3rd, 1410.]

> [JOHN XXIII, May 17th, 25th, 1410–May 29th, 1415.]

MARTIN V, Nov. 11th, 21st, 1417–Feb. 20th, 1431.

EUGENIUS IV, March 3rd, 11th, 1431–Feb. 2nd, 1447.

> [FELIX V, Nov. 5th, 1439–July 24th, 1440–April 7th, 1449.]

NICHOLAS V, March 6th, 19th, 1447–March 24th, 1455.

CALLISTUS III, April 8th, 20th, 1455–Aug. 6th, 1458.

PIUS II, Aug. 19th, Sept. 3rd, 1458–Aug. 15th, 1464.

PAUL II, Aug. 30th, Sept. 16th, 1464–July 26th, 1471.

SIXTUS IV, Aug. 9th, 25th, 1471–Aug. 12th, 1484.

INNOCENT VIII, Aug. 29th, Sept. 12th, 1484–July 25th, 1492.

ALEXANDER VI, Aug. 11th, 26th, 1492–Aug. 18th, 1503 (should be Alexander V, since Alexander V of the Council of Pisa cannot be regarded as a legitimate pope).

PIUS III, Sept. 22nd, Oct. 1st, 8th, 1503–Oct. 18th, 1503.

JULIUS II, Oct. 31st, Nov. 26th, 1503–Feb. 1st, 1513.

LEO X, March 9th, 19th, 1513–Dec. 1st, 1521.

ADRIAN VI, Jan. 9th, Aug. 31st, 1522–Sept. 14th, 1523.

CLEMENT VII, Nov. 19th, 26th, 1523–Sept. 25th, 1534.

PAUL III, Oct. 13th, Nov. 3rd, 1534–Nov. 10th, 1549.

JULIUS III, Feb. 7th, 22nd, 1550–March 23rd, 1555.

MARCELLUS II, April 9th, 10th, 1555–May 1st, 1555.

PAUL IV, May 23rd, 26th, 1555–July 18th, 1559.

PIUS IV, Dec. 25th, 1559, Jan. 6th, 1560–Dec. 9th, 1565.

St PIUS V, Jan. 7th, 17th, 1566–May 1st, 1572.

GREGORY XIII, May 13th, 25th, 1572–April 10th, 1585.

SIXTUS V, April 24th, May 1st, 1585–Aug. 27th, 1590.

URBAN VII, Sept. 15th, 1590–Sept. 27th, 1590.

GREGORY XIV, Dec. 5th, 8th, 1590–Oct. 16th, 1591.

INNOCENT IX, Oct. 29th, Nov. 30th, 1591–Dec. 30th, 1591.

CLEMENT VIII, Jan. 30th, Feb. 9th, 1592–March 3rd, 1605.

LEO XI, April 1st, 10th, 1605–April 27th, 1605.

PAUL V, May 16th, 29th, 1605–Jan. 28th, 1621.

GREGORY XV, Feb. 9th, 14th, 1621–July 8th, 1623.

URBAN VIII, Aug. 6th, Sept. 29th, 1623–July 29th, 1644.

INNOCENT X, Sept. 15th, Oct. 4th, 1644–Jan. 7th, 1655.

ALEXANDER VII, April 7th, 18th, 1655–May 22nd, 1667.

CLEMENT IX, June 20th, 26th, 1667–Dec. 9th, 1669.

CLEMENT X, April 29th, May 11th, 1670–July 22nd, 1676.

Bd INNOCENT XI, Sept. 21st, Oct. 4th, 1676–Aug. 12th, 1689.

ALEXANDER VIII, Oct. 6th, 16th, 1689–Feb. 1st, 1691.

INNOCENT XII, July 12th, 15th, 1691–Sept. 27th, 1700.

CLEMENT XI, Nov. 23rd, Dec. 8th, 1700–March 19th, 1721.

INNOCENT XIII, May 8th, 18th, 1721–March 7th, 1724.

BENEDICT XIII, May 29th, June 4th, 1724–Feb. 21st, 1730.

CLEMENT XII, July 12th, 16th, 1730–Feb. 6th, 1740.

BENEDICT XIV, July 17th, 22nd, 1740–May 3rd, 1758.

CLEMENT XIII, July 6th, 16th, 1758–Jan. 21st, 1769.

CLEMENT XIV, May 19th, 28th, June 4th, 1769–Sept. 22nd, 1774.

PIUS VI, Feb. 15th, 22nd, 1775–Aug. 29th, 1799.

PIUS VII, March 14th, 21st, 1800–Aug. 20th, 1823.

LEO XII, Sept. 28th, Oct. 5th, 1823–Feb. 10th, 1829.

PIUS VIII, March 31st, April 5th, 1829–Nov. 30th, 1830.

GREGORY XVI, Feb. 2nd, 6th, 1831–June 1st, 1846.

PIUS IX, June 16th, 21st, 1846–Feb. 7th, 1878.

LEO XIII, Feb. 20th, March 3rd, 1878–July 20th, 1903.

St PIUS X, Aug. 4th, 9th, 1903–Aug. 20th, 1914.

BENEDICT XV, Sept. 3rd, 6th, 1914–Jan. 22nd, 1922.

PIUS XI, Feb. 6th, 12th, 1922–Feb. 10th, 1939.

PIUS XII, March 2nd, 12th, 1939–Oct. 9th, 1958.

JOHN XXIII, Oct. 28th, Nov. 4th, 1958–.

SELECT BIBLIOGRAPHY

(An asterisk denotes works by non-Catholics.)

ATTWATER, Donald: *The Christian Churches of the East,* two volumes, revised edition 1948, Milwaukee, Bruce Publishing Company.
A Dictionary of the Popes, London, Burns Oates, 1939.

BINCHY, D. A.: *Church and State in Fascist Italy,* Oxford University Press, for the Royal Institute of International Affairs, 1941.

BUTLER, Cuthbert: *The Vatican Council,* two volumes, London, Longmans, 1936.

*CULLMANN, O.: *Peter: Disciple, Apostle, Martyr,* London, S.C.M., and Philadelphia, Westminster Press, 1953.

DVORNIK, Francis: *The Photian Schism,* Cambridge University Press, 1948.

HALECKI, Oscar: *Pius XII,* London, Weidenfeld and Nicholson, and New York, Farrar Straus and Cudahy, 1954.

HALES, E. E. Y.: *Pio Nono,* London, Eyre and Spottiswoode, 1956, and New York, Kenedy, 1954.

HUGHES, Philip: *A History of the Church,* first three volumes, to the Reformation, London and New York, Sheed and Ward, 1934–47.
Pius XI, London, Sheed and Ward, 1937.
A Popular History of the Catholic Church, London, Burns Oates, and New York, Macmillan, 1939.
A Popular History of the Reformation, London, Hollis and Carter, and New York, Doubleday, 1957.

LEBRETON, Jules, and ZEILLER, Jacques: *The History of the Primitive Church,* four volumes, London, Burns Oates, 1942–48, and New York, Macmillan.

MANN, H. K., and HOLLNSTEINER, J.: *The Lives of the Popes in the Middle Ages,* 18 volumes, London, Kegan Paul, and St Louis, Herder, 1928–32.

PASTOR, Ludwig von: *The History of the Popes from the Close of the Middle Ages*, 40 volumes, London, Kegan Paul, and St Louis, Herder, 1937–40.

TOYNBEE, J., and WARD PERKINS, J.: *The Shrine of St Peter*, London and New York, Longmans, 1956.

The Twentieth Century Encyclopedia of Catholicism

The number of each volume indicates its place in the over-all series and not the order of appearance.

TWENTIETH CENTURY ENCYCLOPEDIA OF CATHOLICISM

All titles are subject to change.